The Power of Accepting Yourself

The Power of Accepting Yourself

By

Michael Cohen

Bookline & Thinker Ltd

Bookline & Thinker Ltd
#231, 405 King's Road
London SW10 0BB
Tel: 0845 116 1476
www.booklinethinker.com

A CIP catalogue for this book is available from the British Library.

ISBN: 9780956517760

Cover design by Donald McColl
Printed and bound by Lightning Source UK

To the Memory of Paula Strawbridge

Important Notice

This book is designed to provide information in regard to the subject matter covered. It is not intended to be a substitute for medical or psychological advice or treatment. It is sold with the understanding that the publisher and author are not engaged in rendering psychological, financial, legal or other services. Any person with a condition requiring medical or psychological attention should consult a qualified medical practitioner or suitable therapist.

All client names and cases mentioned have been disguised to protect their privacy and confidentiality.

Table of Contents

Finding Happiness Through Self-Acceptance

My one regret in life is that I am not someone else.
Woody Allen

Do you make assessments of your worth based on such things as how well you perform at work? Or perhaps you consider yourself worthwhile because you have loving relationships with family and friends? Do you measure your value based on your wealth and fame? Or perhaps your acceptability is based on how others judge you.

Bookshops are packed with a plethora of self-help books each recommending that we build up our own sense of self-worth, recognise our inner strengths and focus on our accomplishments.

At first this might seem like good advice. After all, to value oneself is worthwhile and helps people to prosper. Are we not constantly being told that in order to be happy we need high self-esteem?

To esteem yourself means to rate yourself. A person's self-esteem will seem to be high when he is performing well and feeling competent. However, it is all too easy for self-esteem to plummet when a person falls short of his goal, is rejected by a potential partner or feels unworthy when not living up to expectations.

This is how self-esteem becomes conditional and brief, leading people to feel good one minute while condemning themselves the next.

For example, when you achieve success, you may think to yourself: *"I am a good person,"* and when you face a setback you say: *"I failed, and I am a bad person."* We also base self-esteem on how others react to us.

So when you win the approval of significant people in your life, your self-esteem is high and when they reject you it is low.

It is natural to feel good when you perform well. For example, let us suppose that a salesperson gives an excellent presentation to a group of potential buyers. His boss not only congratulates him for closing a lucrative deal but also rates his presentation as one of the most effective he has ever seen.

The salesman feels this makes him a highly capable person and superior to his colleagues. He believes he has earned his high worth and feels good; the better he performs, the better he feels and the higher his self-esteem. The problem with this approach is that our salesman will eventually run into trouble because all people fail at their work some of the time, and our salesman is no exception. As the legendary psychologist Albert Ellis noted: *"When you succeed in getting what you want, you say, 'that is good. Great!' But you also rate yourself and say, 'I am a good person for succeeding!' When you fail to achieve your goals, you say, 'that is bad and I am bad.' "*

According to Ellis, self-esteem is probably the greatest emotional disturbance known to the human race.

So if you make your worth as a person depend on your achievements, your feelings of self-worth will be temporary. Measuring your self-worth in this way will frequently lead to depression and self-loathing whenever you fail to live up to your goals.

In my previous example, the salesperson felt good because his boss congratulated him on giving one of the most effective sales presentations he had ever seen. Winning the approval of his boss can be seen as a good thing – nothing wrong with that; the problem arises when the salesman concludes that because his boss thinks well of him that makes him a good and worthy person. He ties up his worth as a person with his boss's opinion of him.

The following month our salesman gives another sales presentation that fails to secure a deal. This time his boss is very critical, stating that the lack of a sale was primarily due to his inadequate performance.

The salesman's feelings of self-worth plummet. Before even taking the time to think about his boss's opinion, he concludes that because his presentation was inadequate he is inadequate. So our salesman confuses *"an inadequate performance"* with *"being an inadequate person."*

Other examples of this confusion include equating making a mistake with being a mistake; having a failure with being a failure; and doing something that is bad with being a bad person.

This denigration of the self is wrong and a prescription for further failure. If people define themselves as a total failure then they minimise their chances for success in the future. The salesman told himself that he was *"inadequate as a person"* for giving an inadequate presentation. But how could an inadequate person have ever given a presentation that was adequate let alone excellent?

The more people put themselves down, the less likely they are to perform well because they are quite literally prescribing failure for themselves.

How Samantha began to accept herself

A few years ago, a client consulted me with a view to raising her self-esteem. Samantha was due to attend an old school-friend's wedding. She knew that a lot of her old classmates would be there and this was causing her considerable anxiety. Samantha explained that she had been bullied by some of these classmates. She suffered from dyslexia and had considerable difficulty with her reading and writing. This had set her back and she had been placed in a class with students two years below her age. Consequently, these classmates had labelled her the *"school dunce"* and she had felt like one. It had been a struggle, and Samantha took many years to build up her self-esteem.

This articulate and intelligent 39-year-old woman was scared that a meeting with old classmates would bring back these feelings of inadequacy. She thought it unlikely she would again be called a dunce, but would the inference be there? Just the thought of a conversation with them sent waves of anxiety through her body.

I asked Samantha what specifically it was about the reunion that was causing her anxiety.

Samantha worried that her classmates would bring up the subject of their school days. *"What if they start talking about the difficulties I had at school? What if they get drunk and start calling me a dunce again? I couldn't stand that."*

I asked Samantha whose idea it was that she was a dunce?

Samantha: *"I know they used to think I was stupid; they used to bully me about it every day."*

Michael: *"So they used to call you stupid, but does that mean you are stupid?"*

Samantha: *"At the time I used to think it did. I have dyslexia and found reading and writing difficult; it has improved but I still think of myself as a bit thick."*

Michael: *"It sounds like as a child your feelings of confidence and self-worth were low; the bullying and name calling was unacceptable. It must have been difficult to resist agreeing with their idea that difficulty with reading and writing equals stupidity.*

"The good news is that together we can both prove beyond a shadow of a doubt that continuing to hold the view that you are stupid is untrue and self-defeating. Would you like to do that?"

We can see that, at the time, Samantha agreed with her classmates – she had thought of herself as a dunce and still held on to this view today. A popular therapeutic approach to helping Samantha would have been to rehash the trauma of the bullying she experienced in the past and to then focus on her positive qualities in order to raise her feelings of self-worth. To some extent this may have proven helpful. But to focus on her good qualities without addressing the erroneous view she held of herself as stupid would probably have left Samantha with continuing feelings of inferiority. I thought it important to show Samantha that not only were her classmates totally wrong but, more importantly, she was wrong to agree with them.

You are not your problems

Samantha can now see that her dyslexia has been and to some extent still is a problem in her life. It held her back and she left school without any formal qualifications. The mistake Samantha makes is to label herself a dunce.

I asked Samantha to give me a definition of a dunce.

Samantha: *"A stupid person."*

Michael: *"Well that's a definition that we may find in the dictionary; however, I would argue that there is no such thing as 'a stupid person' – just a person who does stupid things. Everyone does stupid things; in fact, I doubt if there is a person in this world who has never done anything stupid."*

Samantha: *"But my classmates thought I was stupid."*

Michael: *"But does that make you stupid?"*

Samantha: *"I believed that dyslexia made me stupid."*

Michael: *"Yes, you did. However, dyslexia is a learning difficulty and having a learning difficulty hardly makes you stupid. Would you consider a person who is colour-blind to be stupid? How about someone who stutters?"*

Samantha: *"If a person says something bad about me I tend to agree."*

Michael: *"That's right – some people will label you; they put you down if you get things wrong, call you all sorts of names, but that's their problem. You can choose not to agree with them."*

Samantha: *"So how do I do that?"*

Michael: *"By never rating yourself as stupid, bad or mad. Rate your traits by all means. For instance, if you were to make a mistake at work you would be correct to think, 'I made a stupid mistake but I am not a stupid person. I am a fallible person who made a stupid mistake.' If I called you an octopus would that make you an octopus – no, of course not. You're a human being, not an octopus, and you're not stupid but a fallible human being who sometimes makes stupid mistakes."*

Samantha was now able to see that rating herself was not only inaccurate but a guarantee of unhealthy emotions such as anger, fear, shame and guilt. You cannot rate people; you can only rate their acts.

The antidote to self-esteem

Self-esteem is a rating game; you rate yourself, your essence and your whole being. This seems fine when life is going well; you have a good career, satisfying relationships and enough money. The problem arises when you tell yourself you're a good person for having these things, because sooner or later life bites you in the bum and things go wrong. You may lose your job, get rejected by your loved one or lose some money; then your feelings of self-worth plummet. The mistake you make is to tie your self-worth up with your success and achievements; and being fallible, like all people, there will be times when you fail.

Surprisingly, the antidote to this trap does not come from some new-age mumbo jumbo but is, in fact, rooted in history. Centuries ago, Greek and Roman philosophers developed the concept of self-acceptance. They saw that in order for a person to be fully self-accepting, it was vital to never rate yourself or other people. The psychologist Dr Albert Ellis has termed this 'unconditional self-acceptance'.

When you refuse to rate yourself, you avoid feelings of anxiety, guilt and inferiority. By recognizing that everyone has shortcomings and that nobody is perfect, you're in a better position to accept your weaknesses along with your strengths. It is healthy to rate your performance, and if you can change something or improve it then so much the better. But if you cannot change it, then accept it and still do as well as you can.

If I was to offer you a £50 note, but before I gave it to you crumpled it up in my hand, would you still want it? Of course you would, because despite being crumpled, it would still hold its true value. However much you may feel crumpled by life, you will always hold your value. So when you fail at something, don't put yourself down and make yourself miserable.

What this book can offer you

The ideas underpinning this book mainly derive from an approach to therapy called Rational Emotive Behaviour Therapy — R.E.B.T. for short. The revolutionary psychologist Dr Albert Ellis developed this highly effective therapy back in the 1950s. R.E.B.T. gets to the heart of emotional problems by showing that unhealthy beliefs cause emotional problems.

Most people believe that when an unpleasant event occurs, that event is responsible for the way they feel. The next chapter shows that this is false. I will show you that it is not events but the rigid and unhelpful way in which you view events that is largely responsible for emotional pain. You will learn to change the way you feel by changing the way you think.

Later in the book, I look at the problem of perfectionism and show you how to free yourself from the prison of perfectionism and how to develop the courage to be imperfect. I then tackle three of the most debilitating emotional conditions in society, which are anxiety, fear and depression. I will teach you how to use self-hypnosis and to relax the mind and body. Once fully relaxed, it's possible to prompt yourself with autosuggestions that will move you forward to greater self-acceptance. I will show you how to set and achieve your goals and how to avoid the pitfalls that block you from getting what you want out of life. Finally, I give you ten ideas that can help you remain positive and enable you to enjoy a successful and emotionally happy life.

At the end of each chapter, you will find some positive statements, or affirmations if you prefer to call them that. If you repeat these to yourself, either silently or out loud, you will move from an intellectual understanding of the ideas to a state where you can believe in them.

My goal in this book is to help you move from self-condemnation to unconditional self-acceptance, and if there is one thing I would like to prove to you beyond all doubt, it is that you never were, never are and never will be a worthless individual.

Major Points

- Never rate yourself. Instead, rate things about yourself. This way you will avoid feelings of anxiety, guilt and shame.
- Your worth as a person does not depend on other people's opinions.
- You can never be a failure: only a person who sometimes fails.
- Never tie your self-worth up with success and achievement, because when things go wrong, your feelings of self-worth will plummet.
- By accepting yourself unconditionally, your emotions will be healthy.

From Head to Heart

Repeat these affirmations to yourself, with conviction either silently or out loud, and you will move from an intellectual understanding of the ideas to believing them.

I do not have to agree with other people's opinions of me.

I will never rate myself, only things about myself.

If I make mistakes, it is not because I am bad or sad but because I am a human being.

How to Change Unhelpful Thinking

There is nothing either good or bad, but thinking makes it so.
William Shakespeare, *Hamlet*

Do you believe that upsetting events in your life are responsible for your negative feelings? If so, you're not alone; this is a popular notion, but it is not strictly true. Adverse events do not cause our emotions to become upset, but our beliefs about those events do.

Let me explain: We probably all experience the frustration of waiting for a late train from time to time. If you look at the commuters on the platform, you may notice some of them getting very worked up. A few may be pacing up and down the platform as though this will magically make the train arrive. Others remain calm, using the time to listen to their iPods or read their newspapers.

This is an example of people reacting to the same event

in an opposite way, with different emotions and behaviours. The passengers who become upset are reacting to the delay in a way that is sure to cause them distress. Most people would assume that their anger is due to the late train, and to a large extent, this makes sense – after all, who likes to be kept waiting? However, this fails to explain why other passengers faced with exactly the same situation remain calm.

To understand the differences in the passengers' attitudes and reactions, we need to look at a model of emotional upset first described by the American psychologist Dr Albert Ellis, the pioneer of Rational Emotive Behaviour Therapy. He calls this the A.B.C. model.

'A' is the activating event, meaning any potentially stressful situation.

'B' stands for beliefs – in other words, a person's thoughts and attitudes about 'A'.

'C' stands for the consequence, i.e., a person's feelings and actions.

The theory behind the A.B.C. model is simple: Feelings are caused more by our thoughts *about* events rather than by the events themselves. According to the model, it is not being kept waiting for a train that is responsible for the passengers' different feelings, but the way they are thinking about the situation.

A commuter remaining calm is probably thinking:

"This is a nuisance but not the end of the world."

"There is not a lot I can do, so I shall have to grin and bear it."

"I might as well relax and make the best of things."

A commuter getting angry is likely to be thinking:

"This train must arrive immediately."

"This is terrible."

"I can't stand being late for work."

In the A.B.C. format, the commuter's situation looks like this:

A   Activating Event: Commuter waiting for a late train.

B   Irrational Beliefs: *"This train must arrive immediately."*

"This is terrible."

"I can't stand being late for work."

C   Consequence: Anger. Body is feeling tense – pacing up and down the platform.

The above beliefs are an example of what Dr Ellis has called irrational thinking and leads anyone who thinks in this way to become angry. Many people would question the idea that these beliefs are irrational. Given the circumstances, wouldn't anyone who is delayed for work think in this way? This is a good question, and in order to answer it, we need to take a close look at the make-up of irrational thinking.

What makes thinking irrational?

The characteristics of irrational beliefs are:

o   They are unrealistic

o   They are rigid

o   They blow events way out of proportion

o   They lead to unhealthy feelings that cause distress

When we hold an irrational belief, we are demanding that events and circumstances be different from the way they actually are by using words such as *"must"* and *"should"*.

E.g. *"I must do well."*

"You should treat me well."

"Life must go the way I demand."

It is not the words themselves, but the attitude behind the words that causes the problem. By making such inflexible demands, we set ourselves up for distress, if – as inevitably happens – life doesn't go quite the way we'd planned.

Many of us also exaggerate the severity of events by using words such as *"awful", "terrible"* and *"I can't stand it"*. Whenever we think in this unhelpful way, we will experience emotional pain such as anger, anxiety, guilt, depression and feelings of inferiority – all are unpleasant.

In the late train example, the angry commuter is holding the rigid belief, *"This train must arrive immediately."* In reality, will demanding that the train arrive immediately make it arrive? Secondly, the commuter is exaggerating the badness of the event by describing it as awful. It is certainly annoying if your train fails to arrive on time, but can it truly be described as awful? Finally, why can't he stand being late for work? In reality, people can stand almost anything.

How to change irrational thinking

To change unhealthy feelings and actions, we need to challenge the way we think by adding 'D' to our A.B.C. model.

'D' stands for disputing and involves vigorously questioning our irrational beliefs. We can do this by asking a number of questions:

D (disputing) What is the evidence for my must/should?

E.g. "*Why must the train arrive immediately?*"

"*Why is it terrible?*"

"*Why is it awful?*"

"*Why can't I stand it?*"

The following example illustrates how to challenge irrational beliefs:

Claire is a secretary who recently lost her job at an advertising company. When she came to see me for therapy, she was feeling depressed and felt it was not worth looking for new employment. Claire thought:

"*I should not have lost my job. I can't stand it. I am totally incompetent and will never get another job like that one again.*"

A. Activating Event: Claire loses her job.

B. Irrational Beliefs: *"I should not have lost my job."*

"I can't stand it"

"I am totally incompetent and will never get another job like that one again."

C. Consequence: Feeling depressed and unable to look for a new job.

After Claire talked the situation though with me, she was able to see that her depression had more to do with her irrational thinking than the job loss itself. In particular, she was doing a first-class job of running herself down. Once she was aware of this, Claire was ready to challenge her irrational beliefs. Here's how she did it:

D. Disputing: Why should I have kept my job?

"Although I would strongly prefer to still be in my job, there is no law that states I should not have lost it."

Why can't I stand losing my job?

"In reality, I can stand losing my job. I have faced difficult situations before and coped. I can cope with this challenge too."

What evidence exists that I am totally incompetent?

"No evidence exists for this idea. I made a number of mistakes while in the job, but that doesn't prove that I am totally flawed – just human. I have done well in past jobs and I can do well again."

What evidence exists that I will never get another job?

"There is no evidence; I am a competent woman with a

lot of skills and work experience to offer. I have found other jobs before and I can do so again."

Rational beliefs

The characteristics of rational beliefs are:

o   They are realistic
o   They are flexible
o   They do not blow events out of proportion
o   They lead to healthy, appropriate feelings

Challenging irrational beliefs helps us form rational beliefs and change the way we feel about an event. By disputing her ideas about the job loss, Claire was able to change her demand that she should not have lost her job into a healthy preference for not losing it. Being unemployed was a setback, but by reminding herself that she had a lot of skills to offer, Claire was able to see that the situation was not awful. She had been in similar situations before and she could find another job again.

Claire was now ready to add 'E' – which stands for Effective new thinking – to the A.B.C. model.

'E' looked like this: *"Although I would have strongly preferred not to have lost my job, I did. I have experienced difficult situations before and managed. I can get through this, too. I succeeded in past jobs and will do so again."*

After changing her thinking, Claire felt sad but no longer depressed. To feel sadness after a job loss is healthy. It would be unrealistic to expect her to feel over the moon given the circumstances. Depression, on the other hand, is an unhealthy emotion and is often an indication that a person is thinking in an irrational way.

The speech that never was

Katie is a successful 28-year-old physiotherapist working in a large practice in London. Liked by her patients and co-workers, Katie has recently been promoted. However, when it comes to socialising, Katie is very shy. She is often asked out to parties by her flatmates and co-workers but more often than not declines. Instead, she spends most weekday evenings watching television and at the weekends goes home to her family in Somerset.

Katie told me about an incident that occurred at a party a number of years ago. It was a good friend's graduation party, and Katie had been asked to make a small speech to congratulate her. Being shy, Katie had always avoided these types of situations however small the crowd. But during her time at university, Deborah had become a good friend and backing out of the speech didn't seem like an option. Katie wrote down everything she wanted to say and rehearsed it many times.

When the time came for Katie to give the speech, her heart started to pound. She opened her mouth to speak but couldn't seem to focus on the words she had written. She felt herself going bright red, her hands started shaking, her heart raced. These feelings overwhelmed her, and she ran out of the room. Katie said everyone was very worried and extremely kind to her but, as far as she was concerned, one of her worst nightmares had become a reality.

Since that party, Katie has felt a total failure; she is still friends with Deborah but rarely goes out to socialise with her.

Katie believed that she had to give a perfect speech and that if she didn't, then she wouldn't be able to cope. The irrational belief Kate held was:

"I must give a perfect speech – if I don't, it'll be awful and I won't be able to stand it."

She also believed that her friends wouldn't accept her if the speech wasn't flawless. Katie was terrified of what others might think or even say about her if her speech wasn't good enough. The demand Katie placed on others was:

"People must think well of my performance; if they don't that proves I am worthless."

Let's join Katie in the middle of her therapy session with me:

Katie: *"I can now see that the belief that I must give a perfect speech led to my anxiety."*

Michael: *"That's correct; when we hold dogmatic, inflexible beliefs, we can quickly develop negative emotions.*

22

You were asking for a guarantee that you wouldn't make any mistakes, yet who can guarantee that? It would have been far better to keep your beliefs flexible with a rational idea such as, 'I would really like to give a perfect speech, but it's not the end of the world if I don't.' "

Katie: *"Oh, I couldn't possibly have done that — I wouldn't want my friends thinking I was worthless."*

Michael: *"Who thinks that you are worthless, you or your friends? Have they told you that you are worthless?"*

Katie: *"No, they haven't."*

Michael: *"Perhaps you believe you're worthless and that you must prove to others that you are not. That is why you demanded that you MUST give a perfect speech. A lot of people think they have to prove they are not worthless instead of starting out with the belief that they are okay."*

Katie: *"Okay, I see that but how could I have stopped myself messing up in the first place?"*

Michael: *"By giving up your irrational belief that you absolutely must give a perfect speech, with no mistakes at all. You put yourself under so much pressure that you virtually guarantee mistakes will occur. A belief is rational when you accept that you're human and allow for the possibility of errors. That way you take the pressure off yourself and you are more likely to make a far more relaxed, genuine speech."*

23

I taught Katie how to use a self-help form to identify, challenge and then change her irrational thinking.

Self-help form

Use the self help form at the end of this chapter and write:

A. Activating Event

Describe the situation – try to be specific.

B. Irrational Beliefs

Identify and write down your irrational beliefs about the event. Remember, irrational beliefs are rigid and contain words such as 'should' and 'must', e.g., *"things must go the way I demand"*. They exaggerate the badness of an event, turning a nuisance into a horror, e.g., *"it's awful/terrible/I can't stand it!"*

C. Consequences

Write down how you felt and acted in relation to the event.

D. Disputing

Vigorously question the validity of your irrational beliefs by asking the type of questions outlined in Claire's example.

E. Effective New Thinking

Write down your new rational beliefs.

F. New Feelings and Actions

Write down how you now feel and act.

Here is how Katie used a self-help form:

A. Activating Event

Giving a speech to congratulate my friend on her graduation.

B. Irrational Beliefs

"I must give a perfect speech—if I don't, it'll be awful and I won't be able to stand it."

C. Consequence

High anxiety; running out of the room.

D. Disputing

Why must I give a perfect speech?

"I would highly prefer to give a perfect speech, however there is no law that states I must."

What evidence exists that I wouldn't be able to stand it if the speech went wrong?

"None — in fact, I have had many things go wrong in my life. I felt very uncomfortable but I am still alive and kicking."

What evidence exists that my friends would think any less of me if my speech wasn't perfect, say for instance, I slipped up on a few words?

"No evidence exists for this idea. I have said things that I considered stupid in the past and not been

rejected."

Even if some of my friends did reject me, would that really be the end of the world?

"No, I would strongly prefer not to be rejected – then again, I wouldn't want to remain friends with people that were so shallow."

E. Effective New Thinking

"I would strongly prefer to give a perfect speech, but I don't have to. If it's less than perfect, it won't be the end of the world. If my friends reject me that would be upsetting but I wouldn't want to remain friends with such shallow people."

F. New Feelings and Actions

Feeling apprehensive but not anxious and worthless. Believe I can talk to my friends about my anxiety in a constructive way.

This is not just positive thinking

You may be familiar with the many books that are available on how to think positively. Positive thinking is a very good idea. In fact, there is now a significant amount of research showing that optimism is an important component of psychological health. However, there is a big difference between rational optimism and the "everything in the garden is rosy" brand of positive thinking. It can be self-defeating and potentially damaging to chant *"every day in every way I'm getting better and better"* while overlooking real problems and issues that need to be addressed. Rational Emotive Behaviour Therapy avoids this potentially damaging form of Pollyanna thinking. Instead of offering positive platitudes, it gets right to the heart of your faulty thinking, helping you to challenge and change unhelpful thoughts with positive but rational thoughts. This changes the way you feel and helps you to achieve your goals.

Negative emotions can be healthy

There are two types of negative emotions: unhealthy negative emotions and healthy negative emotions. Earlier in the chapter, we saw that when Claire lost her job she felt depressed and lacked the motivation to look for another job. Depression is an unhealthy negative emotion and can be the result of irrational thinking. After Claire challenged her negative beliefs about losing her job, she felt appropriately sad and decided to look for another job. Sadness is a healthy negative emotion because it is appropriate to feel sad after an unexpected job loss. When filling out your own self-help form, don't make the mistake of trying to feel good about a negative situation.

Instead, aim to change your feelings appropriately.

Here are some other examples of unhealthy negative emotions and healthy negative alternatives:

Unhealthy	Healthy
Anxiety	Concern
Damning anger	Anger or annoyance
Shame	Regret
Guilt	Remorse
Jealousy	Concern
Hurt	Disappointment

You may be thinking, *"Can a change in my thinking really make a difference to the way I feel? Is it really that easy?"*

The process of filling in a self-help form is indeed quite easy. With some practise, you will soon get the hang of it. Changing the way you feel will take a little longer and require work and practise. You may have to go over your new thinking several times a day, like Katie did. In the following chapters you will learn more techniques to help you. Remember, when under stress most people have a difficult time thinking rationally. You have probably been thinking in irrational ways for a long time. However, by putting in the effort, you will soon find yourself getting less upset.

Major Points

- Adverse events do not upset our emotions, but our beliefs about those events do.
- When we hold an irrational belief, we are demanding that events and circumstances be different from the way they actually are.
- Irrational beliefs are unrealistic and blow events way out of proportion. They lead to unhealthy feelings that cause distress.
- Challenging irrational beliefs helps us form rational beliefs and change the way we feel about an event.
- Rational beliefs are realistic and do not blow events out of proportion. They lead to healthy, appropriate feelings.
- Changing the way you think takes work and practise. Changing the way you feel, react and behave makes it worthwhile.

From Head to Heart

I can enjoy life even though it is not always easy.

It's preferable to have people's approval but I can still accept myself without it.

People will act the way they want, not the way I want them to behave.

I accept myself despite my failings.

<u>SELF-HELP FORM</u>

A. Activating Event
Describe the situation – try to be specific.

B. Irrational Beliefs
Identify and write down your irrational beliefs about the event. Remember, irrational beliefs are rigid and contain words such as 'should' and 'must', e.g. *"Things must go the way I demand."* They exaggerate the badness of an event, turning a nuisance into a horror, e.g. *"It's awful/terrible/I can't stand it."*

C. Consequences
Write down how you felt and acted in relation to the event.

D. Disputing
Vigorously question the validity of your irrational beliefs by asking the type of questions outlined in the examples given in the book.

E. Effective New Thinking
Write down your new rational beliefs.

F. New Feelings and Actions
Write down how you now feel and act.

Claire's self-help form

A. Activating Event
Claire loses her job

B. Irrational Beliefs
"I should not have lost my job."
"I can't bear it!"
"I am totally useless."
"Another job like that will never come along again."

C. Consequences
Feeling depressed and unable to look for a new job.

D. Disputing
Why should I have kept my job?
"Although I would strongly prefer to still be in my job, there is no law that states I shouldn't have lost it."
Why can't I stand losing my job?
"In reality, I can stand losing my job because I have faced difficult situations before and coped. I can cope with this challenge too."
What evidence exists that I am totally useless?
"No evidence exists for this idea. I made a number of mistakes while in the job, but that doesn't prove that I am completely flawed – I'm just human. I have done well in past jobs and I can do well again."
What evidence exists that I will never get another job?
"There is no evidence. I am a competent woman with a lot of skills and work experience to offer. I have found other jobs before and I can do so again

E. Effective New Thinking

"Although I would have preferred not to have lost my job, I did. I have experienced difficult situations before and managed. I can get through this, too. I have succeeded in previous jobs and I will do so again."

F. New Feelings and Actions

Sad but no longer depressed. Able to go out and look for another job

SELF-HELP FORM

A. Activating Event

B. Irrational Beliefs

C. Consequences

D. Disputing

E. Effective New Thinking

F. New Feelings and Actions

For extra self-help forms please photocopy

34

Have The Courage To Be Imperfect

A person who never made a mistake never tried anything new.
Albert Einstein

Does it make you mad if your partner fails to make the bed in the morning? Do you find you're unable to tolerate washing-up left in the sink? These seemingly small matters can eat away at perfectionists and it's possible to literally think yourself into misery. A perfectionist myself, I was given a badge many years ago which read, *"Have the courage to be imprefect"* — with the word imperfect spelt incorrectly. This got me thinking about how difficult it is to make the changes necessary to become a healthy non-perfectionist.

35

To me, perfectionism equals no mistakes, yet I don't know anyone who never makes a mistake. I now realise just how unrealistic perfectionism is. Let's face it, nobody is perfect, and to expect perfection from yourself or others creates unrealistic standards that are likely to create a downward spiral of negative thinking.

This type of thinking leads to self-criticism, and you can end up verbally attacking yourself as well as others. Perfectionists often think in illogical and distorted ways. In his book *Feeling Good – The New Mood Therapy,* Dr David Burns describes ten types of distorted thinking that he refers to as cognitive distortions. Here I give examples of how six of these distortions can manifest in the perfectionist.

All or nothing thinking

A perfectionist tends to see situations in absolute black and white categories; thinking, for example, *"I must be the best or I am nothing."*

Lorraine is a retired secretary who is about to start an Open University degree course in philosophy. She thinks, *"If I don't understand every concept, then this course will be a total waste of time."* It just doesn't enter her head that if she doesn't understand something she can always ask for help, and that if some of the philosophical concepts don't make sense, she can still get enjoyment from the course.

Mental filter

Perfectionists often focus exclusively on negative details, causing their perception of reality to become unrealistic. If they make just one mistake or if someone disapproves of them just once, then it's all gone wrong and anything positive flies out of the window.

After starting her Open University course, Lorraine tells friends that she is learning philosophy. Many congratulate her on going back to education in her later years. However, one person says something mildly critical. What do you think she dwells on – the positive comments or the critical one? Yes, you're right; she dismisses the positive remarks and frets about the negative reaction.

Discounting the positive

In a similar way, when a perfectionist accomplishes something, it's as though it somehow doesn't count. Lorraine's first essay comes back with a good mark, but she tells herself that the essay wasn't that good and was only given that mark by the tutor to encourage her to stick with the course. When another student comments on the high standard of the essay, Lorraine responds by saying anyone could have produced a first essay to that standard.

Mind reading

Perfectionists tend to believe that people are thinking and reacting negatively to them when there is no real evidence to back this up. Lorraine is convinced that her family and friends will think she's crazy to take up studying again after all these years. And she thinks that her sister in particular will wonder what she knows about philosophy. Yet, the fact of the matter is that her sister turns out to be extremely supportive of Lorraine's decision.

Fortune telling

It's common for perfectionists to predict that things will go badly with potentially dire consequences. Lorraine believes that however much effort she puts into studying, she will never gain her degree. *"No matter how hard I try, I just know I'm going to fail,"* she thinks to herself. Yet, realistically, Lorraine has just as much chance of getting her degree as the other students do.

Emotional reasoning

A perfectionist may apply reason based on the way they feel rather than taking the reality of the situation into account. Lorraine believes that her fear of sitting the exam means she will never be able to go through with it. The reality is that she is perfectly capable of passing, but she suffers from exam nerves.

Six Mistaken Ideas of Perfectionism

1. I must be perfect

If you believe you must always be perfect then you'll have a hard time coping with mistakes. Being human means that you sometimes make mistakes. Perfectionists demand that they never make mistakes and spiral into misery when they do. This then leads to anxiety, worry, fears and eventually a "why bother" attitude.

Deborah wants to teach literary skills to adults. Having recently retired, she wants to study for something that she considers worthwhile. An application form from a local college that accepts mature students is sitting on her desk, but she feels anxious so holds back from filling it in.

Deborah is thinking:

o   What if I make a mistake on the application form and don't get accepted onto the course?

o   What if I don't like the course?

o   What if it's all a big mistake?

The real mistake Deborah is making is to demand a perfect outcome. She is asking for a guarantee that she won't make any mistakes, and believes that if she does make an error, it will mean instant failure and rejection. She is also thinking that she might not like the course anyway so why bother.

2. I must be seen to be perfect

Perfectionists often hold the mistaken idea that other people expect perfection of them, when in reality other people expect nothing of the sort. This type of perfectionism is often experienced in social situations. When meeting new people, the perfectionist may be feeling anxious due to the mistaken belief that, *"If you really knew what I was like then you wouldn't want to know me,"* or *"If I shake or blush then you will think I am strange."*

James believes that he has to be the perfect conversationalist and should have the perfect response to any conversation he engages in. James thinks that if he shows a less than perfect understanding of the subject being discussed, people will look down on him. As a consequence, he rarely speaks up, only doing so when he's feeling confident about the topic being discussed. What's more, when he does engage in conversation, he's terrified of how others will perceive him.

James thinks to himself:

o   What if I say something stupid?

o   What if people think I don't know what I'm talking about?

o   What if they look down on me?

James is demanding that he must be the perfect conversationalist, and that if he fails to impress others with his vast knowledge of every single subject, he will be rejected. Is it any wonder that he feels anxious and tends to avoid social interaction?

3. I must control my emotions at all times

Perfectionists sometimes hold the mistaken belief that they must be happy and calm all the time; believing, for example, *"I should never be angry/anxious/ worried/depressed",* or *"I should never argue with anyone".*

Ian has been dating his girlfriend Andrea for three months. During this time, Andrea has called the shots on where to go, who to see and what to do. If Ian suggests they do something different, Andrea tends to dismiss his ideas out of hand. Ian complies with Andrea's wishes, wearing a happy smile and never expressing how he truly feels, but over time, Ian has become increasingly resentful that Andrea never gives his ideas and suggestions the time of day. Ian believes he must play the part of the happy, smiling, compliant boyfriend, but he is becoming increasingly concerned about the future of their relationship.

Ian thinks:
- o   What if she thinks my ideas are no good?
- o   What if we end up having a huge argument?
- o   What if she thinks badly of me?
- o   She might want to dump me

Ian believes he has to hold on tightly to negative emotions and he is terrified of expressing how he really feels for fear of confrontation. He has reached a point where he can't stand it any longer, but rather than tackle the issue, he ends the relationship.

4. My partner must be perfect

Perfectionists sometimes have unrealistic expectations about relationships, and they can have problems sustaining a relationship because they expect perfection from their partner. At first, it may seem like their mate is everything they've been looking for but, as the relationship becomes more involved, they discover that their partner doesn't live up to their expectations. The romantic perfectionist finds it difficult to move from the early honeymoon period to a real human intimate relationship, and they become frustrated and depressed.

Beverly is a serial dater. As an attractive woman, Beverly is asked out by eligible men on a regular basis. However, even though she gets on well with most of them, Beverly just can't commit. After just one or two dates, which is hardly enough time to give her or the guy a chance, she finds something *"not quite right"*. Beverly is unable to choose a mate because she always thinks someone more perfect is just around the corner. As a result, Beverly has never experienced a satisfying long-term relationship.

Beverly thinks to herself:

o   This guy is too fat/thin/short/tall

o   What if he's not perfect in bed?

o   What if he snores?

o   What if I find out he's not perfect?

o   I couldn't stand having to end it

The idea of embarking on a relationship that might not work out terrifies Beverly. In the few relationships that she has had, Beverly has not given much thought to the idea of compromise, and this has stopped her love affairs from progressing. Demanding that a partner is perfect is asking for trouble, and it is no guarantee of a successful intimate relationship.

5. Other people must be perfect

Perfectionists may believe that other people must always meet their expectations, and that they must be perfect. They may also believe that the world must behave in the way they demand, which is a recipe for disaster.

Peter demands perfection from his son, David. He wants him to be the very best in his class. From maths to English, cricket to gymnastics, David has to excel. Peter is totally preoccupied with his son's performance and this inevitably puts David under intolerable pressure. Then, out of the blue, David's head-teacher asks Peter to come into the school to discuss his son's emotional state of mind. It turns out that Peter demands perfectionism from David because he believes it is in his best interest. After all, Peter had been through a difficult time as a child due to his parents' divorce and he had experienced problems at school, which meant that he left school at the age of sixteen without any qualifications.

Peter is thinking:

- ○ He must be the best or else I have failed him
- ○ What sort of a parent am I if I don't push him?
- ○ What happens if he ends up on the scrap heap as I did?

Peter has paid very little attention to David's genuine achievements. Instead of focusing on the fact that David is achieving good grades, he continues to demand an impossibly high standard. This is unintentionally cruel and self-defeating and it is irrational because no one is perfect.

6. In order to be loved and accepted, I must have a perfect body

Holding this or a similar idea may be one of the most potentially damaging forms of perfectionism in our society today, as this leads to an array of problems including eating disorders, depression and even suicide.

Heather is disgusted with herself. Standing on the scales, she has put on 1.5 pounds since yesterday. Heather is sick of the way her stomach sticks out. She's also convinced that her thighs are fatter. Heather resolves not to eat that day and goes off to work determined to drink only water.

She works through her lunch break, but later that day a colleague reminds her about the evening plans for a meal at a local restaurant in celebration of his birthday. Heather's heart sinks and she resolves to have only a salad. When she gets home from the restaurant and sees her bloated stomach, she thinks, *"That's it; I will always be fat."* Reaching into the cupboard, Heather takes out a very large bar of chocolate and devours the lot. She then cries herself to sleep.

Heather is thinking:

- o   I must look perfect
- o   My fat stomach will put men off
- o   Thin is beautiful
- o   If I don't eat today I will lose some of my weight

Heather has some very unrealistic and unhealthy ideas about how to lose weight. She is also very close to developing a serious eating disorder such as bulimia or anorexia. This all stems from her out-of-proportion fear of gaining weight and an unrealistic belief that her body should look a certain way.

Paul: The Driving Perfectionist

Paul has failed his driving test three times. Over the past two years, he has been through four driving instructors and has lost count of the number of lessons he has had. In spite of what instructors have told him, Paul is convinced

45

that he is not cut out to be a driver. *"My instructors keep telling me that I just lack confidence,"* Paul told me when he came for therapy. *"From the moment I get behind the wheel of a car, I get nervous and start making mistakes. How can I expect to get anywhere if I keep messing up?"*

During his first session with me, Paul explains that he is convinced he will never pass his driving test and is contemplating giving up. Despite repeated encouragement from his instructor, Paul believes that when it comes to driving, he is a failure.

Let's join Paul in the early phase of his therapy:

Michael: *"So your driving instructors say you have ability but lack confidence?"*

Paul: *"Well, they're right about the lack of confidence, but wrong about the ability. I think they're just saying that to make me feel better."*

Michael: *"So they're lying?"*

Paul: *"It's just that I get angry with myself when I make so many mistakes."*

Michael: *"That's important and we need to discuss that, but first I would like to ask what you think the instructors meant when they said you have ability. Let's list what you do right."*

Paul: *"Oh they don't really count because of all the mistakes I keep making."*

(Notice how Paul discounts the positive.)

46

At first, Paul is reluctant to contemplate that there are aspects to his driving that are going well. This is a common trait in perfectionists. Although he finds it difficult, he is able eventually to list the things he is getting right and starts to feel a bit better.

Michael: *"So what does this list tell you Paul?"*

Paul: *"OK, I see your point. I'm not a complete failure but that doesn't alter the fact that I get anxious and make mistakes."*

Michael: *"That's true, but your problem isn't the fact that you make mistakes, after all, everyone who has ever learned to drive makes mistakes. Rather the problem is that you demand that you must not make mistakes".*

I explain that when Paul places an unrealistic demand on himself, he generates anxiety, and when feeling anxious we are far more likely to make the very mistakes we're trying to avoid. I explain to Paul the characteristics of irrational beliefs. To recap, these beliefs are unrealistic, rigid and blow things way out of proportion. They lead to unhealthy feelings and behaviours. I tell Paul about the three major irrational beliefs we place on ourselves, others, and the world:

- o I must do well.
- o People should treat me well.
- o Life must go the way I demand.

I then explain three flexible and healthy alternatives to these major irrational beliefs:

- o I very much want to do well but I don't have to.
- o I would prefer that people treat me well, but there is no universal law that says they must.
- o It would be far better if life went as I wanted it to, but there is no guarantee it will.

Michael: *"When you demand that something must be, you are effectively asking for a guarantee. Yet you can no more guarantee zero mistakes than I can guarantee I'll win tonight's lottery."*

I ask Paul what other demands he believes he might be making about his driving.

Paul: *"That I must pass my driving test."*

Michael: *"That's right — again, you are asking for a guarantee and because there are no guarantees your demand is making you feel anxious."*

Paul: *"But I couldn't stand failing."*

I explain to Paul that holding irrational beliefs usually leads to an exaggeration of the severity of events — manifested in the use of words such as *"awful", "terrible"* and *"I can't stand it."*

Michael: *"Let us suppose for a moment that you do fail your driving test again. Why would that be upsetting to you?"*

Paul: *"Because I'd feel like a failure."*

Michael: *"But would feeling like a failure make you a failure?"*

Paul: *"Well it would mean that I had failed my test four times."*

Michael: *"Yes, it would, but there is a world of difference between failing to achieve a goal and being a failure. When you tell yourself that you are a failure, what you're doing is attaching a negative label to yourself. More importantly, you're defining your whole self, your essence, based on a few failed driving tests. Don't you think you're worth more than that?"*

Paul can now see that he has managed to stand failing the test three times, so the chances are he can stand failing again.

Paul's two major demands are:
- o I must not make mistakes
- o I must pass my driving test

I ask Paul to give me a specific example, using the A.B.C. form described in chapter two.

A – Activating Event:

Last Tuesday, during my driving lesson, I was trying to make a three-point turn.

B - Irrational Beliefs:

"I must not screw this up."

"If I do screw this up, it will prove I'm no good and that I will never pass my driving test."

C - Consequence:

Anxiety and feeling worthless.

Let's now take a look at how Paul disputes his irrational beliefs and forms rational beliefs.

D – Disputing:

Is it logical to demand I must not screw this up?

"No, it's illogical. I would highly prefer not to screw up my three-point turn but there's no cast-iron guarantee that I won't."

How does messing up a three-point turn prove I'm no good?

"It proves nothing of the sort. By writing myself off, I am defining myself as no good based on a single mistake."

How does it follow that screwing up my three-point turn means I will not pass my driving test?

"It doesn't follow; while learning to drive, I will probably make many more mistakes before I am ready to take my test. That is how people learn."

After challenging his anxiety-producing irrational beliefs, Paul is ready to write down his new way of thinking.

E - Effective new thinking:

"I would really prefer not to screw up my three-point turn but I cannot guarantee that I won't. During the course of learning to drive, I will probably make more mistakes.

Instead of giving myself a hard time, I will try to learn from my mistakes and improve. That way, I stand a far better chance of passing my driving test."

Reading over his new effective thinking helped change his feelings from anxiousness to mild apprehension, which is a more appropriate emotion.

F - New feelings and actions:

Mild apprehension and looking forward to my next lesson.

Paul had twelve sessions of therapy, during which time we uncovered and challenged his self-defeating attitudes and behaviours. He learnt to challenge his irrational thinking before every driving lesson. Four months later, Paul passed his driving test.

Significantly, Paul had worked on his negative thinking on a daily basis. He also used some of the other techniques described in this book. This is an important consideration, because using one technique on its own will not always be enough to effect a therapeutic change.

Perfection paralysis

Worrying about getting it wrong can sometimes be so powerful that a perfectionist can become paralyzed with fear. If this happens to you, you'll probably find yourself procrastinating and putting off doing something that in reality, you're more than capable of doing. If you feel overwhelmed by a task and fear failure, the following six-point exercise may help.

- o Have a look at the types of distorted thinking I described earlier in this chapter. Are you thinking in "all or nothing" ways? Are you discounting the positive? Are you predicting a potentially disastrous future? Do any of the six mistaken ideas of perfectionism apply to you?

- o Use a self-help form to find out what demands you may be making and ask yourself whether your goals or tasks are realistic?

- o Perfectionists can sometimes set goals that are far too high. Are your goals or tasks achievable, or are you aiming higher than is humanly possible?

- o Break the task down into manageable bite-size pieces, because breaking your goals down into smaller chunks can be really helpful. If you're crossing a river via steppingstones and the stones are too far apart, you may fall in. Bringing those stones closer together means that you can cross it with ease. If you want to write a book but cannot think of the perfect start, remember that the first chapter is only part of the whole book. Who says you can't start writing in the middle?

- o Don't wait to feel like doing something. It's easy to fall into the trap of putting off an important task because you don't feel like doing it. For instance, who do you know who looks forward to vacuuming the house? The truth is that positive feelings follow action. Your sense of achievement comes from carrying out a task.

- o What's the worst that could happen? The perfectionist fears making mistakes and he or she will often perceive dire consequences. Ask yourself what you think might be the worst that could happen? If this does come to pass, what would be the best way of dealing with it? Remember you are only human.

An exercise in imperfection

The following exercise will help you accept the fact that as a human being, you are by nature imperfect. Start by doing small tasks imperfectly. For instance, run your vacuum cleaner over your carpet and deliberately leave a corner of the room untouched, or when doing the washing up, leave a plate unwashed. Some people will find this causes unease – maybe even anxiety – and that's the idea. By confronting your fears, you will discover that nothing terrible happens. You will quickly see that people don't think badly of you or start disowning you. Your anxiety will reduce as you learn that it's all right to be imperfect. As a consequence, you will feel more confident and get more things done.

Major Points

When you expect perfection of yourself, you demand that you never make mistakes.

- o Perfectionism leads to misery, anxiety and worry.
- o Perfectionists will often think in illogical and distorted ways. They will dismiss what they have achieved, focus exclusively on the negative and perceive dire consequences where none exist.
- o If you fear making mistakes, ask yourself, *"What is the worst that could happen?"* Most of the things we worry about never happen. If a worry does come to pass, look for the best way of dealing with it.
- o Ask yourself, *"What demand am I placing on others, the world or myself?"* Use a self-help form to change your thoughts and feelings.
- o Deliberately make a mistake and discover it's okay to be imperfect.

From Head to Heart

I have the courage to be imperfect.

All human beings make mistakes including me.

Making mistakes is a nuisance not a disaster.

Sometimes things only need to be good enough.

Overcoming Anxiety, Fear and Panic

It's not that I'm afraid to die, I just don't want to be there when it happens.
Woody Allen, *Without Feathers*, 1976

Jane feels anxious as the aircraft lurches sharply to the left. For four hours into her flight, Jane has been sleeping like a baby. Now she is wide-awake as the aircraft bumps its way through turbulence. In spite of the reassuring message the First Officer has made, Jane has an uneasy, queasy feeling in the pit of her stomach. Perhaps you have been in a similar uncomfortable situation.

If you believe you are a helpless victim – powerless in the face of anxiety – the good news is that you are wrong. As we have seen in an earlier chapter, it is not external events that cause emotions such as anxiety, but the self-defeating beliefs we hold about those events. For instance, overestimating the danger of a situation while underestimating your ability to cope can cause anxiety. Even though the turbulence only lasts a few minutes, Jane continues to experience anxiety for the remainder of her seven-hour flight. The more she tries to stop feeling anxious, the more anxious she becomes.

Let's join her during a therapy session:

Jane: *"I tried my best to stop feeling anxious. I told myself I had no reason to feel anxiety, that it was only a bit of turbulence and that it would pass. The more I told myself to stop being so stupid and weak, the more anxious I became."*

Michael: *"Telling yourself it is only a bit of turbulence and that it will pass is good advice. However, I think that to demand that you feel no anxiety is counterproductive because you can never have a guarantee of that."*

Jane: *"So does that mean I just have to grin and bear it?"*

I explain to Jane the characteristics of irrational beliefs as described earlier and how unrealistic demands can feed negative emotions such as anxiety. Jane is able to see that she was demanding not to feel anxious. I ask Jane if she is prepared to conduct a little experiment, which she readily agrees to do.

Michael: *"I'd like to ask you not to think of a pink elephant."*

Jane: *"I can see that's impossible – the more I am trying not to think of an elephant, the more the image of an elephant stays in my mind."*

Michael: *"And the more you demand that you must not feel anxious, the more anxiety you're likely to feel. It would be highly desirable not to feel anxious but to force that demand on yourself paradoxically feeds your anxiety."*

After identifying more of Jane's anxiety in relation to flying we fill in a self-help form as follows:

A. Activating Event
Jane's flight experiences turbulence.
B. Irrational Beliefs
"I must not feel anxiety."
"It's just awful to feel anxious."
"I'm too stupid and weak to stop it".
C. Consequence
Rising anxiety – unable to settle for the rest of the flight.
D. Disputing
Where is the evidence that I must not feel anxiety?

"No evidence exists for this – I would highly prefer not to feel anxious but if I do, then I do!"

Why is it awful to feel anxious?

"Well, it's very uncomfortable to feel anxious, but I have coped in the past and I can cope again."

How does an inability to stop feeling anxious make me stupid and weak?

"It doesn't. Many people have difficulty with anxiety. Does that make them stupid and weak? Why the double standard?"

E. Effective New Thinking

"I would really like the anxiety to stop but it doesn't have to stop. Demanding that I must not feel anxious is probably keeping my anxiety alive and kicking. Labelling myself as stupid and weak is not only counterproductive but also factually incorrect. I can distract myself with deep breathing and by listening to some music on the headset. I will then probably find that the anxiety passes."

F. New Feelings and Actions.

Mild discomfort about becoming anxious.

Better able to concentrate on more important things.

By challenging and changing her beliefs, Jane is now able to accept the fact that anxiety (although very uncomfortable) won't harm her. During her next flight, Jane again experiences turbulence. However, having prepared herself by using the self-help form, as well as some of the other techniques described in this chapter, Jane is able to cope with her anxiety.

Don't avoid situations

You may believe it's a good idea to avoid situations you are anxious about. However, nothing could be further from the truth. In many situations, anxiety becomes a learned response. By avoiding those situations you keep anxiety alive. If you make yourself stay in the feared situation you can unlearn your old ways of thinking and feeling, then the anxiety will reduce until it leaves you completely. However, this needs to be undertaken with some care and in gradual steps.

Pam avoids social situations. For her, parties seem like a nightmare. Just the thought of engaging in small talk is enough to make Pam's heart race.

Pam repeats many of the "what ifs" experienced by sufferers of social anxiety. *"What if I say something stupid? What if they think badly of me? What if I shake and spill my drink? What if people walk away from me? What if I get tongue-tied?"*

After identifying and challenging Pam's irrational ideas, we decide to draw up a hierarchy of the fears Pam experiences at social gatherings on a scale of 0% to 100%, with 0 representing no anxiety and 100 the most anxious she can feel. It looks like this:

A friend's house-warming party

Situation	Anxiety Level
1. Getting ready to go to the party	10%
2. Walking into the party with a friend	20%
3. Saying hello to the host	35%
4. Being offered a drink	40%
5. Someone asking me to pass him a drink	45%
6. My friend walks away to talk to someone else	50%
7. Being introduced to someone I have never met before	60%
8. Being asked my opinion in front of several people	90%

Picture yourself coping

As you can see, Pam's list is graded from getting ready to go to the party at just 10% anxiety to being asked her opinion in front of several people at a massive 90% anxiety.

I introduce Pam to coping imagery. I ask her to imagine acting like a calm and confident version of herself. Pam pictures herself coping with the situation. She starts by picturing herself getting ready to go to the party. This causes her very little anxiety so we move on to her arriving at the party. Pam reports feeling a little anxiety but she feels as though she is coping relatively well. Once she starts to picture herself saying hello to the host she starts to feel anxious.

In order to reduce Pam's anxiety, I ask her to use the breathing exercise that I explain later in this chapter. She also silently repeats a positive coping statement developed from her self-help form. After some practise, Pam is able to reduce her anxiety from 35% to 0%.

Then Pam moves on to the next scene in which she imagines someone offering her a drink.

Michael: *"Close your eyes, take three deep breaths and in your mind imagine someone offering you a drink."*

Pam: *"I have the image and my instinct is to say no. If I accept the drink, I am bound to shake and show them all just how anxious I really am. However, I am going to imagine accepting the drink and coping."*

Michael: *"That's good, but before you imagine accepting it, take in three deep breaths and repeat your coping statement:* **'I have been worried about shaking many times before and coped. I will cope again.'** *"*

Pam: *"I am picturing myself. I am a little anxious but I am accepting the drink – I can see myself coping."*

After practising this technique a number of times, Pam reduces her anxiety from the original 40% all the way down to zero, no anxiety. She is ready to move on to the next level.

During the time we work together, Pam receives a number of social invitations that give her the opportunity to practise the skills learnt in therapy. Pam is pleasantly surprised to discover that the coping imagery has given her a new-found confidence. Although she experiences some anxiety it is reduced to the extent that she is able to enjoy herself, something she has not done at a party for many years.

How to use coping imagery

Here, in a nutshell, are the instructions for drawing up your own hierarchy of fears and using coping imagery to overcome them.

○ Decide the issue you wish to work on. It may be a fear of flying, a job interview, a sales presentation or a social event like Pam's party.

○ Go through the stages of the event and draw up a hierarchy of fears in the same way Pam did, from 0% (no anxiety) up to 100% (the highest amount of anxiety you can experience).

○ Find a comfortable place to sit, uncross your arms and legs, and then close your eyes. Take three deep breaths and visualize yourself in the situation with the lowest level of anxiety on the hierarchy.

o   You may find that, at the lowest level on the scale, you experience little or no anxiety. If there is no anxiety, move on to the next level. If you do experience anxiety, do the following: Take slow comfortable deep breaths through your nose, breathing out through your mouth. Feel your body relaxing. Breathe in slowly and evenly through your nose, exhaling even more slowly through your mouth.

o   As you breathe in, silently say the word "calm" to yourself. As you breathe out, say the word "relax". Try to make the out-breath up to twice as long as your in-breath. The idea is to empty your lungs of old air and make room in your lungs for fresh oxygen-rich air. One way to achieve this is to slow down the speed you repeat the word *'relax'*. *'Calm'* on the in-breath, *'R-e-l-a-x'* on the out-breath.

o   Imagine yourself in the situation again seeing things though your own eyes. Take the feelings of relaxation with you into the scene. Imagine acting like a calm, relaxed and confident version yourself. Go though the whole scene and imagine yourself handling things in a calm and confident way.

o   You may also find it helpful to silently repeat a positive coping statement. You can use or adapt one found at the end of each chapter in this book or you may want to create one of your own, perhaps developed from the effective new thinking on your self-help form.

Practise your coping imagery until you reduce the percentage of anxiety to zero, then move on to the next level using the same technique.

It will take practise to reduce the anxiety experienced at every level of your hierarchy – but it will be worth it. I would encourage you to get out into the real world and face your fears. This will take courage but you can do it. Pam did just that and is now leading a confident and happy social life.

Whatever can go wrong, will!

David's relationship with Mel is getting serious. Mel's parents have invited them both over for dinner. David, being a traditional man, feels the need to ask Mel's father for permission to marry his daughter. Mel's father is a professor of physics. David is a plumber, without an academic qualification to his name. David has made up his mind that the meeting is going to be a disaster.

He imagines Mel's father looking over his spectacles with disapproval, asking what gives him, a plumber, the right to marry his beautiful, educated daughter.

Mel tries to reassure David that her parents are kind, accepting people and his job will not be an issue. However, Mel's reassurance makes no difference and David continues to focus on an extremely negative outcome. This is often referred to as catastrophising and occurs when a person expects the worst to happen, blowing it way out of proportion. It occurs also when people tell themselves a situation is unbearable or awful, when it is really just uncomfortable or a nuisance. Blowing things out of proportion can stop a person from taking on new challenges because they only focus on failure.

When David comes to see me, he is thinking of turning down the invitation, feigning illness. It is understandable that David feels apprehensive about meeting his prospective in-laws and asking for permission to marry Mel.

However, what makes it awful? Where is the evidence that Mel's father will disapprove of David? Even if he were to disapprove, can it truly be described as 100% terrible? After all, Mel has pointed out that she will marry David without her father's blessing.

The emotional Richter scale

The seismic activities of earthquakes are measured on the Richter scale. A great way to drastically reduce catastrophic thinking is to measure catastrophising on an emotional Richter scale.

Emotional Richter scale

Not bad   The worst an
                                                     event could be

0%---10-------30-----50----70-------90---100%

On a scale of 0 to 100, I ask David to place an X on the spot that indicates how bad he feels it would be if Mel's father disapproves of their intention to marry.

David puts an X at 95%, which is very high.

                              Mel's father disapproves
                                        ↓
0%---10-------30-----50----70-------90---X--100%

I then ask David what could happen that would be worse than being rejected by Mel's parents. David replies that he could be run over on the way to meet Mel's parents.

I ask him if, in the unlikely event that he was run over, where he would place the X on the scale.

David places the X at 100%.

I then ask David what could be worse than this, to which David replies that he could die as a result of being run over. David then tries to add another 10% to the scale to represent the seriousness of dying. When I explain to David that nothing can be higher than 100% bad, he realises he will have to re-evaluate the seriousness of the previous examples by lowering the other two Xs on the scale.

I continue to ask David for other examples of what could be worse than being rejected by Mel's parents. We get as far as a nuclear bomb going off in Mel's parents' garden. Amid tears of laughter at the thought of a nuclear bomb exploding in a physics professor's back garden, David is now able to see that he was exaggerating the severity of being refused permission to marry Mel. He also concludes, as Mel had implied, that if her father were to be so unreasonable, he wouldn't have to take it seriously.

After our work, the emotional Richter scale looks like this:

Mel's father disapproves of our intention to marry

Nuclear bomb in garden

↓ ↓

0%---10---x----30-----50----x70------x-90--------x100%

↑ ↑

Being run over   Dying

By writing down some examples of worse but unlikely things that could happen, David is able to see how he has been blowing the event out of all proportion. The following summer David and Mel marry, and her father gives her away.

If you find yourself exaggerating the terror of a situation, use the emotional Richter scale to put things into perspective. Ask yourself: *"Am I overreacting? Would it really be that terrible?"* This can lower your anxiety considerably.

Panic attacks

James thinks he is about to go mad – the train has stopped moving and has been between stations for the last five minutes. The train operator has not bothered to make an announcement. James feels his heart pounding. He thinks he is about to have a heart attack. Feelings of terror start to take over. James thinks that at any moment he will be compelled to open the door of the train and run. *"What will the other passengers think of me if I make a dash for the door? Perhaps they can see my panic. Why is everyone else so calm?"*

The train starts moving and James begins to relax.

James suffers from panic attacks, an aspect of anxiety.

If you have ever experienced a panic attack, you will know how terrifying it can seem. James's symptoms include a pounding, rapid heartbeat with shortness of breath, pains in the chest and a compulsion to flee the place where he is experiencing the attack. James sums it up by stating that he thinks he is about to lose control and go mad. Other typical symptoms of panic include sweating and shaking, tingly or numb fingers, nausea and intense fear. During a panic attack, people often experience feelings of unreality as if they are in a dream-like state. All of these feelings are scary but not unusual. In fact, when experiencing a panic attack these feelings are normal.

What is a panic attack?

A panic attack begins with a false alarm. It is as if your mind tricks you into believing that the situation and the symptoms you are experiencing are dangerous. James really is terrified on that stationary train and truly feels that he is about to die of a heart attack. Of course, in some situations we need to be alerted to impending danger. If you are in a building that is on fire or are confronted by a vicious animal, you need a signal that warns you of the danger. Fortunately, nature has provided this and it is called the fight or flight response.

Faced with a threat, the body reacts immediately with a rush of adrenaline, heightened muscle tension, faster heart rate and raised blood pressure. Blood pumps to the muscles and brain, causing the body to become alert and as strong as possible. This is because, in order to survive, you need to respond by either fighting the threat or running away from it

– an appropriate response if your life is being threatened by a real emergency.

Fortunately, we are rarely faced with life-threatening situations. Being stuck on a train is very unpleasant for James but hardly life-threatening.

How a panic attack develops

You may believe that a panic attack comes out of the blue. One minute you feel relatively calm, the next you are overwhelmed with the most intense feelings of anxiety. However, there are several aspects to a panic attack and understanding them is the first step in stopping them.

The first stage involves a physical sensation such as a feeling of unease, pressure in the chest, a heart flutter or a sense of dread. These feelings are followed by thoughts that predict dire consequences such as:

"What if I am having a heart attack?"

"I'm going to die."

"If I don't get out of here, I will go mad."

These beliefs seem very real and lead to a rise in anxiety. This then leads to further catastrophic thinking, which notches up the anxiety until a vicious circle of anxiety and catastrophic thinking brings on a full-blown panic attack.

Although you're only too aware of the feelings of anxiety, you may be unaware of your catastrophic thinking.

However, it is there, camouflaged in the feelings of dread.

The Stop Technique

Thought-stopping is a technique first introduced by a man named Bain in his 1928 book and further developed by behavioural therapist Joseph Wolpe in the 1950s. It is primarily used for the treatment of obsessive thoughts and phobias. It can be adapted to ease anxiety by adding some extra elements and works as follows:

○ As soon as you feel the slightest feeling of unease, say the word *"Stop"* to yourself — if you're on your own, you may find it more effective to say it out loud. If you're in the company of others, say it silently but with passion, as if you are saying it aloud. You can say it with as much force as you like. One of my clients also imagines a cannon being fired at the same time. Some people imagine a red traffic light. You can add to the word *"Stop"* phrases such as *"Stop, this is nonsense"* or *"Stop, I don't need this."* However, don't make the mistake of putting yourself down. It is the catastrophic thoughts and feelings you are silencing, not yourself.

○ Next, focus all your attention on external sights and sounds in your immediate vicinity. For instance, James fixes his attention on the train's route map just above the train door. Jane, our airline passenger, scans passengers looking for an attractive male. Another of my clients, Alice, experiences panic while working on the computer and so focuses her complete attention on the report she is typing. In this way, you give your mind something external to focus on, instead of your negative thoughts and feelings. Use as many of your senses as you can – sight, sound, smell, even taste – to bring yourself into the present moment.

o   Next, use a breathing technique to calm yourself down. Breathe in slowly and evenly through your nose, exhaling even more slowly through your mouth. As you breathe in, silently say the word *"calm"* to yourself. As you breathe out, say the word *"relax."* Try to make the out-breath up to twice as long as your in-breath. The idea is to empty your lungs of old air and make room in your lungs for fresh oxygen-rich air. One way to achieve this is to slow down the speed you repeat the word, *"relax"*.

"Calm" on the in-breath, *"R-e-l-a-x"* on the out-breath. If your mind wanders, bring your attention to your words as you breathe in calm and out r-e-l-a-x-e-d.

Exercise can help

Exercise can reduce and relieve symptoms of anxiety and panic. Performed on a regular basis, physical activity helps to reduce excess adrenaline and also increases the morphine-like substances found in the body that have positive effects on mood. Swimming, fast-paced walking, running or riding a bicycle are wonderful ways of ridding the body of excess adrenaline. Many people report a sense of well-being after they have exercised. If you have not exercised for some time, it is important to start moderately and gradually build up. It's also advisable to see your doctor before embarking on an exercise program.

Don't avoid your emotions

Do you tend to bottle up your true emotions, holding back what you really think and feel? When someone upsets or angers you, do you refrain from saying anything for fear of conflict? Research suggests that suppressing emotions often leads to anxiety and panic attacks.

Sometimes people hold back their emotions out of fear, and this can then lead them to feel anxious. One common belief is: *"In order to be accepted, I have to be liked and get along with everyone all the time."*

To achieve this unrealistic expectation, a person will try to please others, often ignoring their own feelings and needs. They also avoid conflict at all costs for fear of upsetting other people.

Another related self-defeating belief is: *"I must be happy and cheerful all the time."* The person believes that she is not allowed to feel negative emotions. She may believe that feelings such as anger are unacceptable, even dangerous. Rather than express these feelings, she suppresses them. However, powerful emotions such as anger often find a way of being expressed indirectly as anxiety and panic.

Nina has experienced anxiety and panic most of her adult life. She tells me that the previous week she hosted a dinner party for some good friends. Half-way through the dinner she was struck with a panic attack that came right out of the blue. The panic attack was so powerful that her husband had to ask their friends to leave and that was the end of the party.

Nina enjoys hosting dinner parties and doesn't have a clue what triggered the attack. However, she is now worrying that future parties will bring on further anxiety and panic. I ask Nina if anything had happened before or during the party that may have triggered the attack. At first she insists that nothing had happened. However, after further questioning, Nina relates that her friend Patricia had asked if she could come over to help her prepare some of the dishes. Patricia was about to start a catering business. She was due to cater for her first client the following week but Patricia spent most of the time criticising Nina's cooking. This climaxed with the comment, *"Never mind, Nina, you do try but you can never come up to my professional standards."*

I ask Nina how she felt about Patricia's comments.

Nina tells me that Patricia had taken the trouble to come over and help, so she felt she couldn't make a fuss and upset her. After further discussion, Nina realises that she had, in fact, felt extremely insulted and angry with Patricia but held back from acknowledging this, even to herself. We discover that whenever Nina feels strong negative emotions such as anger and rage, she holds on to these feelings for fear of upsetting people. Instead, she smiles and is the nice, charming person she thinks others expect her to be.

When emotions are not acknowledged and expressed they can manifest themselves in the form of anxiety and panic. I refer to this as the body speaking its mind. Once Nina has identified, understood and acknowledged the cause of her anxiety, it is time to do something about it.

If anxiety and panic attacks seem to come out of the blue with no apparent explanation, ask yourself:

- o Is there a problem situation or feeling that I am not addressing?
- o Perhaps someone or something has upset me?
- o Work towards a resolution of the issue. This could be as straightforward as expressing how you feel. It may require you to speak to someone who has upset you to resolve the conflict.

Effective communication

Expressing how you feel is important. You need to get things off your chest. However, like Nina, you may have reservations about speaking up. Some simple but effective communication skills will enable you to be assertive and get your point across while minimising the possibility of conflict.

By standing tall, yet still being open and relaxed, you will be making a stand through your posture. You will also be communicating to the other person that you are confident.

Don't smile too much or nod too much.

Maintain direct eye contact instead of looking down at the floor.

Because people can react negatively to criticism, it can be helpful to cushion the blow by starting with a positive statement, as the following example illustrates:

"I really appreciate your offering to help but I feel upset by your remark."

This example also illustrates the use of 'I' statements instead of 'you' statements.

'You' statements are far more likely to cause the other person to become defensive. 'I' statements are a way of communicating an issue without accusing the other person of being the problem.

Contrast the following:

'You' statements
"You always have to be asked to do the washing-up."
"You never think things through."
"You never finish your work on time."

'I' statements

"I would be very grateful if you could help me with the washing-up".

"I would really like you to think about that before rushing into anything."

"I am getting held up with my work, as I don't have that report yet. Can you tell me when it will be ready please?"

Nina resolves her issue with Patricia

During therapy I help Nina face her fear of confrontation. Over a number of sessions, she practises her assertiveness skills by role-playing difficult situations such as the one she faces with Patricia. Nina plays the role of her critical friend and I respond using some of the communication styles listed above. Then the roles are reversed with me being the confrontational friend and Nina responding using the skills she has learned.

The following Sunday, Patricia comes over to see how Nina is feeling after her panic attack. After some initial small-talk Nina speaks up:

"I really appreciate your coming over to see me today. However, I need to tell you that I felt undermined at my own dinner party by the comment you made about my ability to prepare the dishes. I would really appreciate it if, in the future, you keep such comments to yourself."

Patricia responds by apologising. She says that she had been feeling anxious and a little overwhelmed about starting up her new business. She honestly feels that Nina is a more experienced cook than she is and didn't mean to upset her. They remain the best of friends.

Learning to confront rather than avoid difficult emotions can take time. Maybe you can enlist the help of family and friends as you practise your new communication skills and assertiveness. You can also practise being assertive in front of a mirror, in your imagination and by recording your new communication style and playing it back. You will get it wrong sometimes but that is because you are human. With practise you will succeed.

Major Points

o Do not avoid situations in which you experience anxiety. Instead, gradually expose yourself to the feared situation. That way you will unlearn your old ways of thinking that feed the negative feelings. Anxiety will then reduce until it leaves you completely. However, this needs to be undertaken with some care and in gradual steps.

o A panic attack begins with a false alarm. It is as if your mind is tricking you into believing that the situation and the symptoms you are experiencing are dangerous when they are not at all.

79

- o Exercising on a regular basis will reduce your anxiety and panic. It is a powerful form of relaxation that increases the morphine-like substances found in the body. These have positive effects on mood.

- o Research suggests that suppressing emotions often leads to anxiety and panic attacks. Instead of bottling up your true feelings, learn to become assertive and confront rather than avoid difficult emotions. This may take some time but will be more than worth it.

- o Use techniques such as coping imagery to overcome your anxiety. Find a comfortable place to sit, uncross your arms and legs then close your eyes. Take in three deep breaths and visualise yourself coping. Start with the situation you fear least and work towards more challenging situations.

From Head to Heart

Anxiety is an old habit pattern that I can and will change.

Panic attacks may feel dangerous – but that doesn't make them dangerous.

I've stopped my negative thoughts before and I'm going to stop them again now.

Right now I have feelings I don't like but they will soon pass.

Heal Depression

The mind is its own place, and in itself can make a Heaven of Hell, a Hell of Heaven.
John Milton (1608 – 1674)

Depression is a common emotional disorder affecting around half the adult population at some point in their lives, with many people suffering from severe depression. Make no mistake – clinical depression is an illness, and it is one of the most painful mood states that can be experienced.

We all have our down days, but the intense feelings of sadness associated with depression can last for weeks, months and even years. There is a vast difference between feeling down in the dumps and being depressed. The symptoms of depression can be both emotional and physical, and can seriously affect a person's ability to function. It's not uncommon for people to think of depression as a sign of weakness and to label themselves as useless. It is especially painful when a well-meaning person says *"pull yourself together,"* because this is exactly what the depressed person wishes he or she could do, but can't.

Symptoms of depression include:
o   Feelings of hopelessness
o   Loss of interest in life
o   Fatigue
o   Difficulty concentrating
o   Lack of motivation
o   Lack of self-acceptance
o   Feelings of guilt
o   Negative thinking
o   Suicidal thoughts and feelings
o   Disturbed sleep
o   A change in appetite - overeating and under-eating
o   Weight change
o   Loss of libido

If you're experiencing some of these symptoms, you may be depressed. However, it's important to resist the temptation to self diagnose. Depression requires medical and psychological evaluation. If you are feeling depressed, then please make an appointment to see your doctor. This book gives you useful and proven tools for dealing with depression, but it is not a substitute for competent medical and psychological care and therapy. Assuming you have heeded my advice, let's look at some ways to help relieve depression.

How to cope with depression

Withdrawing from the world

Laura believes her life is falling apart. Her two-year relationship recently ended and she blames herself. But rather than move on, she sits at home refusing to make social arrangements with friends because she thinks they'll see her as a failure and perhaps side with her ex. When people do telephone, she imagines they're just getting in touch out of pity.

Laura also thinks she's about to lose her job. As an advertising executive, she's meant to be out seeing clients, but over the past six weeks she's only managed to visit five contacts. She's not bringing in new business and this compounds her feelings of inadequacy and depression.

Laura has been referred to me for therapy after being diagnosed with depression. She ruminates about what went wrong in her relationship, believing that if she had *"just tried harder"* it would have worked out. It's important that she talks through her thoughts and feelings about the ending of her relationship so that negative emotions don't become bottled up inside. Laura also wants to get back to work, but she finds it hard to concentrate and doesn't have the energy. Her apathy is causing her a lot of guilt because she can't understand why she's so unmotivated.

During her first therapy session, Laura begins to understand that her negative thinking, low energy levels and poor concentration are by-products of her depression. She has always been an enthusiastic and motivated worker, and her apathy is out of character. Laura agrees to give herself some time to heal before returning to work. She explains the situation to her employers; they understand and are kind to her, so they give her the time to get better.

Plan your day

Laura tells herself that it's not worth doing anything, and activities like cleaning the house or going for a walk are just too difficult. One of the first things Laura and I do is plan a daily activity schedule. This involves Laura writing down activities for the day. I explain to Laura that if she plans what to do and when to do it, she will find it easier to become more active and this will help decrease negative thinking. In addition, doing even the most straightforward activities improves motivation and leads to a greater sense of achievement. These activities need to be practical, realistic and pleasurable. This is what Laura's activity schedule looks like:

Laura's weekly activity schedule

	Mon	Tues	Wed	Thurs	Fri	Sat	Sun
9-10	B'fast	B'fast	B'fast	B'fast	B'fast	B'fast	B'fast
10-12	Laundry	Dust	Vacuum	Walk	Shop	Walk	Walk
12	Tea	Tea	Tea	Tea	Tea	Tea	Tea
1	Email	Email	Email	Email	Email	Email	Email
1-2	Lunch	Lunch	Lunch	Lunch	Lunch	Lunch	Lunch
2-4	TV	IT	IT	TV	TV	IT	Friends
4-5	Exerc	Walk	Exerc	Walk	Exerc	Walk	Friends
5-6	Supper	Supper	Supper	Supper	Supper	Supper	Snack
6-8	TV	Friend	Walk	TV	Walk	Friend	Walk
8-10	Read	Read	Read	Read	Read	Friend	TV
10	Bed	Bed	Bed	Bed	Bed	Bed	Bed

If you find it difficult to get going and everyday activities feel like a Herculean task, you may find it beneficial to draw up an activity schedule like the one above. It's important not to overload yourself with too much activity, though. As you can see from the illustration above, Laura has drawn up her activity schedule over a week. Each day is marked off into segments. By allocating specific times to tasks, people find they gain a sense of control over their day and their motivation to do things starts to come back.

Stop putting yourself down

If you're experiencing depression, you're probably aware that your thinking is overly negative and unrealistic. Perhaps you evaluate yourself in the worst possible light. Maybe you put yourself down and blame yourself for things that are not even your fault. You may interpret your present situation and future as hopeless and tell yourself that you have nothing to look forward to. Regardless of the type of depression, your thoughts play an important role in maintaining and even deepening your depression.

Laura first met Douglas in one of the restaurants that he owns. She said, *"I was with some colleagues from work, and Douglas came over to our table to ask if everything was all right. We got talking and he asked me out."*

Laura said that Douglas worked long hours running his two restaurants, but that he had time for Laura at the beginning. After three months they bought a flat together. However, a few months down the line things started to go wrong.

The restaurants stopped doing well, and Douglas became increasingly withdrawn and moody. Laura had been left a sum of money after her grandmother died, and Douglas asked for a loan of the money to help support his flagging business. Laura was uneasy about doing this, but Douglas was manipulative and he used emotional blackmail to get his way. Against the advice of family and friends, she lent him the money. Douglas's business deteriorated, and he became bankrupt. Then Laura learned that the bank had a charge over their flat and that they were going to lose it as part of the bankruptcy. As we delved further into Laura's past relationships, it soon became apparent that she has a tendency to fall in love with manipulative and controlling men. Let's join Laura during a therapy session with me:

Michael: *"You're finding it difficult to accept the fact that Douglas has left."*

Laura: *"I can see that he did a bad thing by taking my money and mortgaging our flat up to the eyeballs to support his business, but I feel half a person without him."*

Michael: *"How does his leaving you make you half a person?"*

Laura: *"Well I feel sorry for myself and just sit at home – I don't want to see my friends."*

Michael: *"Do you think you may be telling yourself that you need him even though he has behaved in a pretty appalling way?"*

Laura: *"Yes, that's it. I mustn't lose him."*

Michael: *"Perhaps you need to ask yourself why you need him. Why must you not lose him?"*

Laura: *"I don't feel worthwhile unless he's there."*

Michael: *"It sounds like you're saying you're less of a person without him. But how does his not being with you make you worthless?"*

Laura: *"Well, I'm not sure – I just feel worthless I suppose. I haven't really questioned it."*

Michael: *"That's right. You think and tell yourself that you're incomplete and a worthless person – and how can a worthless person go out and face the world? However, let me ask you, does feeling worthless make you a worthless person and does not being with Douglas truly make you incomplete?"*

Laura: *"I am beginning to see what you're driving at."*

Michael: *"You see, Laura, you're rating yourself. You're saying to yourself that you're only a worthwhile, acceptable person when you're with Douglas."*

Laura: *"Thinking about it, I have felt that way about relationships and myself for a long time – I only feel good enough if I am with a man."*

Michael: *"So do you think you put up with some pretty lousy behaviour from some men just to be with a partner?"*

Laura: *"Yes, because the idea of being left is awful. I don't want to be alone."*

Michael: *"Being on your own does have its disadvantages but can it truly be described as awful or terrible? And is it worth putting up with being treated badly just to be with someone?"*

Laura: *"Well, maybe not awful, but I don't feel good on my own."*

Michael: *"Does being on your own make you less of a person?"*

Laura: *"No, I suppose it doesn't."*

From this we can see that Laura is measuring her self-worth by her relationships. She defines herself as worthless when she is on her own, but worthwhile and complete when she is in a relationship. Being without a partner is to Laura proof of her worthlessness and this leads her to sit at home with a "why bother?" attitude. After all, if she sees herself as worthless, why bother doing anything?

Michael: *"So Douglas leaving you is proof that you're worthless."*

Laura: *"Well if I look at it like that it does seem a bit ridiculous – but that is how I feel."*

Michael: *"You feel worthless because you tell yourself you're worthless – so what is it about you that makes you a worthless person?"*

Laura: *"I see myself as unacceptable to Douglas."*

Michael: *"And what is it that's unacceptable about you?"*

Laura: *"I argued about giving him the money to help him out of his financial difficulties and I shouted at him when*

I found out he had used our flat as a guarantee against his business."

Michael: *"Okay, let me see if I understand you. In order to be accepted you have to agree with everything Douglas demands of you and you're not allowed to become upset and express your anger?"*

Laura: *"Well, again, when I look at it that way it is a bit stupid. But if I do express how I feel then, like Douglas, other men may pack up and leave."*

Michael: *"Yes, they might; and because you see yourself as worthless and incomplete without a partner you demand a guarantee that they mustn't leave you, but look at the price you pay for that. You don't allow yourself to express your feelings. You go along with everything that is asked of you regardless of how unreasonable and damaging it is for you. But, despite paying this price, does it really guarantee that a partner won't leave you?"*

Laura: *"If I really look at it, no. However hard I have tried to hold on to a partner, they leave – in fact, friends have told me I try too hard and that this puts men off."*

Michael: *"If you truly believe you must be in a relationship, and that if he leaves you then that proves you're worthless, then you may try desperately to keep your partner no matter the cost to you."*

Laura: *"But being left is awful. I just can't stand it."*

Michael: *"What makes it awful, Laura?"*

Laura: *"Being on my own and not being invited out by friends, who are surely thinking, 'Oh here we go again. She can't keep a relationship going.'"*

Michael: *"That's what you tell yourself they think, but have they told you that's what's going through their minds?"*

Laura: *"Well, no."*

Michael: *"So it's your idea, not theirs. You tell yourself that your friends will think of you as inadequate and worthless – however, you have no proof that they think that way. Even if they did, would that make them right? You see Laura, you are defining yourself as unworthy. You're telling yourself that without a man, you are unacceptable and unworthy and others would be right to see you that way. You are trying to gain your worth through the acceptance of a man and the acceptance of friends. That causes you problems. You're demanding a guarantee of acceptability, yet it can never be guaranteed – people may accept you today, but will they accept you tomorrow? If you keep hold of that philosophy your self-worth will go up and down like a yo-yo, and you will constantly be trying to please a partner and friends at all costs."*

Laura can now see that she was defining herself as unacceptable when she had no partner and concluding that, because she saw herself that way, others would see her too. Rejection by a partner is very unfortunate and it is part of life but it is hardly the end of the world.

Laura may have future relationships that end, and she may conclude it is her fault that she is on her own. This would not make her an unacceptable person but a fallible human who makes mistakes. If people disapprove of Laura, she can work on accepting herself in spite of their disapproval and focus on making improvements and forming new relationships.

Let's look at Laura's beliefs in the A.B.C. self-help form:

A. Activating Event

No matter how hard I try, Douglas leaves.

B. Irrational Beliefs

"This proves I am a worthless, unacceptable person."

"I can't bear being on my own!"

"People will think I am totally worthless, and they're right."

C. Consequence

Feeling depressed and unable to face the world.

Now let's see how Laura challenged her irrational beliefs:

D. Disputing

How does Douglas leaving make me an unacceptable person?

"It doesn't make me unacceptable, but trying to gain my worth through the acceptance of a man or friends is

irrational and causes me problems. I can accept myself in spite of Douglas leaving."

Why can I not stand being on my own?

"In reality, I can stand being on my own. I would prefer to have a partner in my life right now, but I can stand not having one, especially one like Douglas."

What evidence exists that people will think I am worthless, and even if they did think that, would it make them right?

"No evidence exists that people think I am worthless — that's my idea, not theirs. Even if they did think I was worthless, it wouldn't make me worthless. I don't have to define my self-worth according to other people's opinions of me."

Laura is now ready to add her effective new thinking. This is what she wrote:

E. Effective New Thinking

"I would prefer to be in a relationship at this time but I don't have to be. Regardless of what others think, I can choose to be happy and to accept myself, whether I am in a relationship or on my own."

Laura's new feelings and actions were:

F. New Feelings and Actions

Felt sad and disappointed about the end of the relationship but not depressed — more energy and better able to engage with friends.

Over the next few months, Laura attended weekly therapy sessions and worked very hard at changing her attitude towards herself, her friends and her relationships. She has returned to work and has recently started dating again.

Laura had some pretty irrational ideas about the *need* for a relationship. She defined herself as unacceptable without a partner, concluding that because she saw herself that way, others would too. When a relationship ends, it is natural to feel sad. You may not have the same issues as Laura, but if you have long periods of depression, it is possible that you may be engaging in unrealistic and unhelpful thinking. With the aid of the self-help form, look for the irrational beliefs that are contributing to feelings such as hopelessness, guilt and worthlessness. With work and practise, you can change these beliefs.

Some powerful tips for combating depression

Get active

Often the last thing a depressed person feels like doing is exercise. However, exercise really can make you feel better because it releases endorphins, the body's natural anti-depressant hormone. Do a form of exercise you find enjoyable. Swimming, walking or riding a bicycle are wonderful ways of relieving depression. I have found that depressed clients really benefit from fast-paced walking, as it gets them out of the house, requires little in the way of preparation and needs no special exercise equipment.

Make your exercise aerobic by walking briskly but be gentle with yourself. Start gradually and build up the amount of exercise. Don't expect to be an Olympic champion! Perhaps you can join an aerobic or swimming class.

When starting any form of new exercise, it is always advisable to consult your doctor first. If you experience chest pain or any other distressing symptoms, seek medical attention.

Distract yourself

People who are depressed often describe having self-critical, guilty or negative thoughts. We have talked in some length about strategies to challenge negative thinking. Another powerful strategy is to ensure your mind and body are busy – for example, you could make a phone call and talk to someone you trust. Communication is important and can help distract you from your internal dialogue.

You can take yourself to the shops or the park, making sure to look around you and observe passers-by, animals, even the trees. If the weather is bad, try playing a game on the computer, or pop some music on and do the housework.

By becoming engaged in an activity, you move your attention away from your internal chatter to the external world around you.

Show contempt for your negative, irrational thoughts

It is important to identify and challenge your irrational thoughts. However, sometimes it's enough to just ignore them.

If you find yourself ruminating over your irrational thinking, see the thoughts for what they are – negative and unhelpful. Your time is important and you have important things to do. Giving these thoughts attention is a drain on your time and resources.

Avoid alcohol and illegal drugs

It's imperative to totally avoid alcohol as well as illegal and some non-prescription drugs. Alcohol and illegal drugs affect the body's central nervous system and can cause depression. What's more, they inhibit the effectiveness of anti-depressant medication as well as some other medicines

There is also some evidence to suggest that products containing aspartame, such as sweeteners, can make symptoms of depression worse. If in doubt, speak to your doctor.

Seek out the sun

Get as much sunlight as possible. Sunlight has been shown to have an anti-depressant effect, even in the UK. Don't be put off because it's overcast – as long as there is some light, it can have a positive effect.

Manage your eating habits

Depression can affect your eating habits. You may find you lose your appetite or you lack the motivation to prepare food. Some people find their appetite for unhealthy foods increases and they end up gaining weight. Both of these habits tend to exacerbate depression. Blood sugar levels can go up and down and can affect your mood, making you feel even more miserable. Eating regular meals will help to stabilize your blood sugar level and your mood. Aim for three meals a day – breakfast, lunch and an evening meal, with a healthy snack mid-morning and mid-afternoon to boost your metabolism and ensure energy is used effectively.

If you find it hard to eat, try eating little and often. People who have issues with food will need to keep a check on irrational thinking. For instance, perfectionism about body image, as well as an "all or nothing" approach to dieting can contribute to depression.

Keep a diary

Take some time each day to write a diary. This can include writing down your thoughts about the positive and negative aspects of each day. This helps you learn what you feel depressed about and what makes you happy, or at least distracts you from your depression. After a week or so, read over your diary and you may find what you need to do to lift your mood and what you need to avoid doing to prevent your depression from getting worse.

Practise mindfulness

Mindfulness involves focusing your mind on the present. You become aware of your actions in the present moment. You don't judge – you just observe. This is a simple concept but it is quite challenging. It is natural for our minds to judge our experiences as good, bad or neutral. Start by paying attention to an everyday experience without drifting into thoughts of the past or worries about the future. The idea is to not be caught up with thoughts or opinions about what's going on. Here are some tips:

- o Stand still or sit down and simply pay attention to your breathing. Focus on the sensation of the air moving in and out of your body, as well as the rising and falling of your diaphragm and chest. Notice the

99

air entering your nostrils and leaving your mouth. Don't judge, just observe.

o Observe your thoughts – simply watch them come and go. These may be thoughts of worry, anxiety, despair or optimism – don't ignore them or fight them, just observe them without judgment.

On other occasions, you should become mindful of everyday tasks such as making the bed – notice the feel of the quilt, the smell of fresh sheets or the movement of your hand as you make the bed. When you focus your awareness on the here and now, you reduce worries, relieve stress and improve your mood.

You may find it beneficial to take a course in mindfulness meditation. By being "present in the moment" you can reduce the symptoms of depression, stress and even physical pain.

How to get a good night's sleep

A common problem associated with depression is sleep disturbance. Some people find they cannot get to sleep; others wake frequently, while some sleep for far too long.

The majority of people seem to benefit from between six to ten hours of sleep a night. However, some people can cope well on far less, especially as they get older.

It is not necessarily the amount of hours you sleep but how you feel the next day. The following are tips that can help you get to sleep and stay asleep.

Set yourself a bedtime and an awakening time

Set yourself a time to go to bed and get up. This way your body will get used to falling asleep and waking up at certain times. If you go to bed at different times, or have naps during the day, you lower your chances of a good night's sleep. However tempting it is to nap, remember that sleeping during the day can affect your ability to sleep at night. There is even some research to suggest that a nap during the day can negatively affect your mood.

Reduce and avoid sleep-disturbing substances

If you are depressed, I strongly suggest avoiding alcohol, as it is a depressant. However, if you do drink, avoid doing so at least five to six hours before bedtime.

Some people drink alcohol because it has a sleep-inducing effect. The problem arises when alcohol levels in the body start to fall as this induces a "wake up" effect. Caffeine drinks such as tea, coffee, cola and some energy drinks can keep you awake at night.

Again, I would recommend reducing your intake and avoiding caffeine at least five to six hours before bedtime.

101

The five to six hour rule should also be applied to rich, spicy and sugary foods.

Exercise helps you sleep

Exercise is good for you. It helps heal depression and can deepen and improve the quality of your sleep. However, vigorous exercise close to bedtime is not a good idea as it may stimulate you and interfere with sleep.

Use self-hypnosis and relaxation techniques

Self-hypnosis and relaxation techniques as described in this book can help you get to sleep. You can use them before bedtime and while in bed to help relieve anxiety and relax your mind and body.

Make your bedroom conducive to sleep

Making your bedroom a cozy place to sleep gives you the best chance of getting a good night's rest. Is the room too hot or cold? Is your bedding comfortable? Are you using too many or too few pillows?

Reducing noise in the room and cutting out as much light as possible will help. Avoid the temptation to read or watch television as your bed should really only be used for sleeping and sex.

Prepare yourself for sleep

Avoid worrying or dwelling on stressful issues just before bedtime. A warm relaxing bath before turning in can help induce sleep. You could include some essential oils, though do seek the advice of a doctor or qualified therapist, as they should not be used if you are pregnant, if you take certain medicines or if you have certain medical conditions. A warm milky drink and a light snack just before bed can also help. If you find you don't fall asleep within 20-30 minutes, don't lie in bed tossing and turning; instead get up, go into another room and read until you feel sleepy.

Major Points

You are NOT weak

Make no mistake – clinical depression is an illness and it is one of the most painful mood states that can be experienced. It requires medical and psychological evaluation. The symptoms can be both emotional and physical and seriously affect a person's ability to function. It is the illness itself that can lead you to think of depression as a sign of weakness and to label yourself as useless.

Change your thinking

Regardless of the type of depression that you're experiencing, your thoughts play an important role in maintaining and even increasing your depression. Use the self-help form and look for irrational beliefs that may be contributing to feelings such as hopelessness, guilt and worthlessness. By identifying and challenging your irrational thoughts, you can change them.

Distract yourself

Keep your mind and body busy. Pick up the phone and talk to someone you trust. Take yourself to the shops, or the park, and be sure to look around you and observe other people, animals and trees. By becoming engaged in an activity, you move your attention away from your internal chatter to the external world around you.

Practise mindfulness

You should practise mindfulness by paying attention to everyday experiences. Don't drift into thoughts of the past or worries about the future. The idea is to not become caught up in thoughts or opinions about what's going on. Focusing your awareness on the here and now will help to reduce worries, relieve stress and improve your mood.

Talk to other people

Talk to family and friends about how you feel. Never think of yourself as a burden. You may be surprised to discover that others have felt depressed themselves and understand how you feel.

Look after yourself

It is essential to look after yourself even in good times, but this is especially important when experiencing emotional difficulties such as depression. If you're finding it difficult, ask your partner or a close friend or relative to help you eat well and avoid alcohol, caffeine and illegal drugs. Treat your negative thoughts with contempt, embrace the sunlight and take regular exercise. To feel well, you need to eat well, exercise well and sleep well.

From Head to Heart

It is okay to ask for help and support from my family and friends.

I will not put myself down regardless of how I am feeling.

In order to feel well, I need to eat healthily, get active and sleep well.

Self-affirmation will help me while self-condemnation will hinder me.

I will make a special effort to accept myself at this time.

How to Use Self-Hypnosis

What is self-hypnosis?

Have you ever seen old horror films and television programmes that portray hypnosis as a frightening instrument of mind control where unscrupulous villains enslave the will of helpless victims?

Perhaps you have seen stage shows where a hypnotist appears to use "hypnotic powers" to make people do and say things that they would never do under normal conditions. If so, it is not surprising that hypnosis may seem just a little bit wacky, not unlike other seemingly mystical and unexplainable phenomena.

This is unfortunate because hypnosis is a serious therapeutic tool that can help people overcome psychological, emotional and even some physical problems.

Hypnosis is not:

- o Mind control
- o Brain-washing
- o Sleep
- o Unconsciousness
- o A peculiar altered state
- o A mystical state

When in hypnosis a person is:

- o Aware
- o In control
- o In a natural and harmless state
- o Can come out of hypnosis when he or she wishes

The state of hypnosis can best be described as a state of highly focused attention with heightened suggestibility. Hypnosis is sometimes (but not always) accompanied by relaxation. When a therapist induces hypnosis in another, it is called hetero-hypnosis and is often referred to as clinical hypnotherapy. When hypnosis is self-induced, it is called autohypnosis and is often referred to as self-hypnosis.

The word hypnosis comes from the Greek word hypnos which means 'sleep'. It is an abbreviation of the term neuro-hypnotism or nervous sleep which means sleep of the nerves.

This term was used by the eminent neurosurgeon James Braid (1795-1860). However, hypnosis is not a sleep state. In fact, when in hypnosis, a person is awake and usually aware of everything that is said and done.

How can I use self-hypnosis to achieve my goals?

Self-hypnosis is often used to modify behaviour, emotions and attitudes, so many people use self-hypnosis to help them deal with the problems of everyday life. Self-hypnosis can boost confidence and even help people develop new skills. A great stress and anxiety reliever, it can also be used to overcome habits such as smoking and overeating. Sportsmen and women can enhance their athletic performance with self-hypnosis, and people suffering from physical pain or stress-related illnesses also find it helpful (hypnosis should only be used in this way after a medical diagnosis has been made and under the guidance of a doctor or qualified therapist).

A self-hypnosis technique

I am going to introduce you to a simple but effective technique for self-hypnosis. Eye fixation self-hypnosis is one of the most popular and effective forms of self-hypnosis ever developed. We will start by using it as a method to help you relax. After you have practised a number of times, we will add hypnotic suggestions and imagery.

Reduce distractions by going into a room where you are unlikely to be disturbed. Turn off your phone, television, computer, etc. Avoid eating a large meal just beforehand so that you don't feel bloated or uncomfortable. Unless you wish to nod off, sit in a chair, because lying down on a bed will likely induce sleep. You may also wish to loosen tight clothing and take off your shoes. If you wear contact lenses, it is advisable to remove them. This is your time. You are going to focus on your goal of self-hypnosis and nothing else.

1. Sit in a comfortable chair with your legs and feet uncrossed.
2. Without straining your neck or tilting your head too far back, pick a point on the ceiling and fix your gaze on that point.
3. While you keep your eyes fixed on that point, take a deep breath in and hold it for a moment, and then breathe out.
4. Silently repeat the suggestion: *"My eyes are tired and heavy and I want to SLEEP NOW"*
5. Repeat this process to yourself another couple of times, and if your eyes have not already done so, let them close and relax in a normal position.
6. It is important that you say the suggestions as if you mean them, for example use a gentle, soothing but convincing manner.
7. Let your body relax.

8. Allow your body to become loose and limp in the chair just like a rag doll.

9. Slowly, and with intention, count down silently from five to zero.

10. Tell yourself that with every count you're becoming more relaxed. Stay in this relaxed state for a number of minutes while focusing on your breathing.

11. Notice the rising and falling of your diaphragm and chest.

12. Be aware of how relaxed your body is becoming without you even having to try. In fact, the less you try the more relaxed you become.

13. When ready, come back to the room by counting up from one to five in a lively and energetic manner.

14. Tell yourself that you are becoming aware of your surroundings and, at the count of five, you will open your eyes.

15. At the count of five, open your eyes and stretch your arms and legs.

Repeat this technique three or four times and notice how each time you reach a deeper level of relaxation. However, if you find you do not relax as much as you would like, do not force it. There is a learning curve involved so resolve to practise self-hypnosis on a regular basis

Sometimes people will feel a little spaced out or drowsy after they come out of hypnosis. This is similar to awaking from an afternoon nap. It is harmless and passes after a few moments. However, do not drive or operate machinery until you feel fully awake.

Difficulties learning self-hypnosis

Have you ever experienced the frustration of having a name on the tip of your tongue? The harder you try to remember the name, the harder it is to recall. Then when you relax the name comes back to you. Sometimes, when we try too hard, we block ourselves from achieving our goals. The attitude you take towards self-hypnosis will determine how easily you learn it. Don't try too hard or set unrealistic goals. Relax and take your time. Accept the pace at which you achieve results, however small they may appear at first. Believe in yourself and you will go on to achieve the success you desire.

Post-hypnotic suggestions and their rules

As previously mentioned, hypnosis is a state of heightened suggestibility. Suggesting something when in hypnosis will enable an action or other response to take place after the hypnotic experience has occurred. These suggestions are called post-hypnotic suggestions, and they will help you to achieve your goals. Over the years, hypnotherapists have developed rules of suggestion. These are guidelines that will enable you to achieve maximum success with the suggestions you give yourself. What follows is a summary of these guidelines.

Say it as if you mean it

Have you ever seen an actor mumbling his lines on stage, speaking in a quiet meek voice? The result is a performance that isn't very convincing. Unlike acting, hypnotic suggestions are often repeated silently. However, you need to repeat the suggestions as though you mean what you say. Be reassuring, positive and confident.

Suggestions need to be phrased positively and in the present tense

Most of us will react more favourably to a positively worded suggestion than a negative one. Which request would you rather hear: *"Don't leave that shirt lying on the floor"* or *"Would you mind picking that up?"*

Suggestions are far more effective when you say what you wish to move towards, rather than what you wish to move away from. For example: *"I am calm,"* is better than *"I am not anxious." "I can stop smoking with ease"* is better than *"I will try to stop smoking"* as the word *try* implies difficulty and struggle.

Your suggestions are best phrased in the present tense, as though they are happening at this moment in time. So, *"I am relaxed on the aircraft"* is better than *"I will be relaxed* when I am on the aircraft" or: "I am becoming more confident" is better than "I will try to be confident," which implies something that you might be able to do at some time in the future.

Make your suggestions specific and realistic

Your suggestions will be more effective if they are specific and realistic. If you wish to improve your swimming performance, it would be unrealistic to give yourself the suggestion: "I am a world-class swimmer," unless of course you are, or are about to become, a world champion. Instead, ask yourself what specifically it is about your swimming that you wish to improve. Thus, if you wished to improve your breaststroke, you would give yourself a realistic suggestion tailored to that specific aspect of your swimming. Structure your suggestions on the changes you wish to see in yourself rather than things that are out of your control.

Do not give yourself suggestions for two or three issues all at the same time. For instance, the suggestion, "I am confident that I can lose weight and stop smoking," is probably not effective. Instead, work on one goal at a time, repeating suggestions associated with that goal. When you see some results, move on to your next goal.

Repetition of suggestions

Advertisers know the value of suggestion, which is why they repeat television and radio commercials on a regular basis. One of the most important rules when practising self-hypnosis is repetition of your suggestions. That way you drive the point home and are far more likely to effect positive change.

Imagery in hypnosis

While giving yourself hypnotic suggestions, visualise the situation, the action and the feeling that you desire. As well as picturing a desired outcome, you can utilise your sense of touch, hearing and even smell. You can create new images as well as using images from your memories and experiences.

People sometimes believe they have to see a crystal clear image of their goal, as though watching a movie. However, a positive attitude and a belief that you are in the role are more important than clear imagery.

The following exercise will illustrate how effective suggestion and imagery can be. Do not use this image if you have an aversion to lemons.

The lemon example
- o Sit down in a comfortable chair and close your eyes.
- o Picture an ordinary lemon.
- o Imagine you are cutting this lemon in half.
- o Observe the juices running down each piece of the lemon.

- o Pick up a piece of the lemon. Bring it up to your mouth and bite into it.

Even if your image of the lemon wasn't clear, you might still have grimaced or even found your mouth watering.

Adding hypnotic suggestion and visualisation to self-hypnosis

Rehearsing positive outcomes

Mandy experiences stage fright. She is due to take part in a play and is anxious that her performance will not be up to her highest standard. Mandy wants to learn self-hypnosis to help her feel more confident. I teach Mandy self-hypnosis and then teach her results imagery. In this technique, the person visualises herself performing and reacting in the way she desires while repeating post-hypnotic suggestions to help achieve a goal. After putting herself into hypnosis, Mandy pictures herself on stage performing with confidence and ease. While visualising this for thirty seconds, she repeats three times the post-hypnotic suggestion, *"I am performing with ease and confidence."* While still in hypnosis, she repeats this process two more times.

The Technique

- o Sit in a comfortable place with legs and feet uncrossed.

- o Without tilting your head or straining your neck, pick a point on the ceiling and fix your gaze on that point. While you keep your eyes fixed on that point, take a deep breath in and hold it for as long as is comfortable. Then, as you breathe out, repeat the suggestion: *"My eyes are tired and heavy and I want to SLEEP NOW."* Repeat this process to yourself another couple of times and, if your eyes have not already done so, let them close and relax in a normal closed position.

- o Allow your body to become loose and limp in the chair just like a rag doll. Then, slowly and with intention, count down silently from five to zero. Tell yourself that with each and every count you're becoming more and more relaxed.

- o Picture an image that represents a situation you wish to master and see yourself achieving your goal.

- o Repeat to yourself three times a positive suggestion such as: *"I am confident, calm and relaxed."* Say this with conviction while picturing the image for about 30 seconds. Repeat this three times, while staying in hypnosis and focusing on your body's relaxation.

- o Come back to the room by counting up from one to five and opening your eyes.

How to set your self-hypnosis goals

o Give achieving your goals a high priority. Plan to use self-hypnosis on a daily basis and you will begin to see results.

o Write your goals down on paper. Clarify what you want to work on and be specific. Make sure you set goals that are achievable. If they are long-term goals, it may be helpful to break them down into manageable steps.

o Formulate your hypnotic suggestions and write out a number of suggestions for the goal you are working on. Follow the rules of post-hypnotic suggestions. You may even want to write your own script (see the example further down).

o Decide on the imagery you plan to use. If your aim is to relax, picture a pleasant scene like a beach or a park on a warm summer's day. You may wish to use results imagery, as Mandy did.

o If you fail to achieve a goal, do not give yourself a hard time. Remember, failing to achieve a goal does not mean you are a failure. It may be that you need to approach the goal in a different way or perhaps you need to be persistent.

A self-hypnosis script to help you relax and reduce anxiety

Below is a sample script designed to help you relax and cope with anxiety. Feel free to alter the imagery to fit your particular needs. For instance, instead of picturing yourself on a beach, you may prefer to imagine that you are in a park on a warm summer's day. You may also wish to change the symbolism.

It is probably best to record the text and play it back, or have someone read it to you.

First, take yourself into hypnosis by:

o   Sit in a comfortable place with legs and feet uncrossed.

o   Without tilting your head or straining your neck, pick a point on the ceiling and fix your gaze on that point. While you keep your eyes fixed on that point, take a deep breath in and hold it for as long as is comfortable. Then, as you breathe out, repeat the suggestion: *"My eyes are tired and heavy and I want to SLEEP NOW."* Repeat this process to yourself another couple of times and, if your eyes have not already done so, let them close and relax in a normal closed position.

o   Have a friend read this to you, or play the tape you previously recorded:

119

"I am now allowing my body to become loose and limp in the chair just like a rag doll. As I continue to relax, I am noticing where the comfort is in my body. I notice a warming comfortable feeling in my hands and fingers or maybe the comfort is noticeable in another part of my body. With every breath that I take and every sound I hear, the comfort deepens. I now count down from five to zero. With each and every count, my relaxation deepens. It may even double. Five - deeper - four - calmer - three - more relaxed - two - one - zero.

I now picture myself on a golden sandy beach. I can feel the warmth of the sand under my feet and the warmth of the sun on my body. I imagine that I am alone on the beach or that others are there as my relaxation continues. I listen to the sound of the sea, the waves lapping against the shore. I feel so calm, secure and relaxed that I can stay on the beach for as long as I choose. After a while, I picture myself in a field on a warm summer's day. There is not a cloud in the sky. In the middle of this field is a hot air balloon and attached to the balloon is a basket that is weighed down on the ground with sandbags. The hot air balloon hangs effortlessly in the sky. I now imagine that I am placing any worries, fear or anxieties into the basket. The more I offload my worries into the basket, the more relief I feel. I now feel as if a great weight has been lifted from my shoulders.

I release the sandbags and watch as the balloon, along with its basket, rises into the air. As I watch the balloon rising into the air, I feel relief. The higher the balloon rises, the more relief I feel. The more distant the balloon becomes, the more insignificant my worries appear to be. As I watch this balloon getting smaller in the distance, I repeat to myself three times:

'I am letting go of my worries, fear and anxiety.'

When ready, I come back to the room by counting up from one to five and opening my eyes."

When you practise self-hypnosis, the imagery you use and the suggestions you give yourself are only limited by your imagination.

Main Points

Hypnosis is a serious therapeutic tool, which can be used to help people overcome many psychological, emotional and even some physical problems. It is not mind-control, brainwashing, sleep, unconsciousness or a peculiar, altered or mystical state. When in hypnosis, a person is aware, in control and can come out of hypnosis when he or she wishes to. It is a natural and harmless state.

Self-hypnosis can modify behaviour, emotions and attitudes. It can be used to increase confidence and develop new skills. It can help to reduce stress and anxiety, and it can even help people overcome habits such as smoking and overeating. Self-hypnosis is also used by sportspeople to enhance their athletic performance. If you are experiencing any medical or psychological problems, however, it is essential to seek the advice of a doctor or competent therapist before using self-hypnosis.

Avoid eating a large meal just before practising self-hypnosis so that you don't feel bloated or uncomfortable. Unless you wish to doze, sit in a chair, as lying down on a bed will likely induce sleep. You may also wish to loosen tight clothing and take off your shoes. If you wear contact lenses, it is advisable to remove them. Keep your legs and feet uncrossed.

Remember, failing to achieve a goal does not mean you are a failure. It may be that you need to approach the goal in a different way or perhaps you need to be persistent.

Practise self-hypnosis on a regular basis. Relax and take your time. Accept the pace at which you achieve results, however small they may seem at first. Believe in yourself and you will go on to achieve the success you desire.

Post-Hypnotic Suggestions

Here are some post-hypnotic suggestions you can use in your self-hypnosis. Feel free to alter them to fit your particular needs.

- o *Each and every day I am calm, secure and relaxed.*
- o *I am becoming more assertive and confident when I speak to colleagues.*
- o *Each and every day I accept myself as I am.*
- o *Each and every time I enter hypnosis I relax more deeply.*
- o *I find it easy to stop smoking.*
- o *I eat three healthy meals a day.*

How to Reach Your Goals

If you don't like something change it; if you can't change it, change the way you think about it.
Mary Engelbreit

Stephanie believes her life is a total mess. A smoker and overweight, Stephanie tells me that she has being trying to cut out cigarettes and lose weight for years. Stephanie starts a diet with good intentions but always seems to sabotage it after a few weeks. She has the same experience when trying to stop smoking. Stephanie is doing a first-class job at running herself down, labeling herself a failure, weak and stupid. She also has some nasty names for herself – 'fat slob' being just one.

Let's join Stephanie during the early stages of her therapy session:

124

Michael: *"You seem to be doing a first-class job of running yourself down."*

Stephanie: *"Well, I am just a total waste of space, a real failure! I start a diet, stick to it for a few weeks, then I just seem to give in to temptation."*

Michael: *"So you have had a difficult time sticking to a diet but you seem to think this difficulty with dieting makes you a failure. Can you see how this idea probably blocks you from getting back on track with your diet?"*

Stephanie: *"I do tend to feel bad about myself and give up. Then it takes me a good few months before I start another diet."*

Michael: *"Instead of labeling yourself 'a failure,' it would be better to look at the triggers that lead you to sabotage your diet. Wouldn't this give you a better chance of avoiding making the same mistake next time?"*

Stephanie: *"Yes, I hadn't looked at it that way."*

From this short conversation, Stephanie is able to see how holding a view of herself as a failure is counterproductive and leads to a "why bother" attitude. She has discounted the fact that on many occasions, she had stuck to her diet for two weeks or more before she had given in to temptation. When it comes to dieting, Stephanie demands perfection, and that is something that is impossible to achieve. When she does slip up, she labels herself negatively, rather than understanding that she has simply made a mistake and that she can get back on track with her diet. In Stephanie's eyes, a mistake equals total failure. This is "all or nothing" thinking. However, after some time Stephanie can see how it is possible to make a mistake, accept herself and then get back on track with her diet.

Setting goals doesn't mean demanding perfection

You start with the best of intentions – going on a diet or starting an exercise program. Then you slip up. Perhaps you eat more than you planned or miss the gym two days running. Do you feel that this "mistake" somehow proves you're weak and pathetic? Do you then conclude that your diet or exercise program is not worth bothering with? If so, can you see how this attitude is self-defeating? If you ask fifty people who have successfully lost weight if they stuck to their diet 100 percent of the time, you would be hard pressed to find one who did. The same is true of people who maintain a successful exercise program. Wanting to do the best you can is a positive attitude, and it feels great to achieve your goals. The problem comes when you demand that you MUST achieve your goals all the time, every time, 100 percent of the time. The problem with this attitude is that when you make a mistake and don't achieve great results, you may conclude that you are an inferior person.

When setting goals, adopt the attitude that you're going to do the very best you can. If you make a mistake, view it as an opportunity for learning. Doing something without demanding that you 'must' succeed all of the time takes some of the pressure off and, paradoxically, this can lead to a greater chance of success.

Steps to Goal Setting

Step one - decide what you want out of life

Many people are dissatisfied with their life situation. They know that they want things to change but they are not clear exactly how. The first step you need to take is to decide what it is you want out of your life. Do you want to develop intellectually, get a new job or improve your finances? Maybe you want to improve your health, start a new hobby or even go on a spiritual journey.

Start by making a list of your dreams. Don't be afraid to write them all down. Where do you want to be in two or five years from now? You could start by asking yourself "What needs to change?" If that doesn't get the grey matter working and you need a bit of motivation, ask yourself the somewhat more radical question: *If I thought I was going to die in 18 months, what would I like to do with the time I have left?*

Step two - prioritise your goals and be specific

You may now have a formidable list of goals. Now is the time to prioritise. Decide which goals are the most important to you. Write *one* for the most important, *two* for the next and so on. Once you have listed your goals, you need to be specific and state them clearly. This way you will be able to measure your progress effectively. For instance, if one of your dreams is to start your own business, you need to ask yourself what sort of business you wish to start and when you want to start it.

A specific goal may look like this: *"I will start my own secretarial service this April and devote three days a week to working at home."*

Your goals need to be within your own control, not outside of it. For instance, the goal: *"I want my flat mate to do some of the housework instead of expecting me to do it all,"* means that the goal rests with the flat mate and that is perhaps wishful thinking. Instead, set the goal as: *"I will learn assertiveness skills and challenge my flat mate about the issue."* This puts the goal within your control.

Step three - a plan of action

In order to move forward with your goal you need a good plan of action. Without a plan, you may find your goals get confused and you become disheartened. Knowing what steps you are going to take in the process of reaching your goal is important for lasting change. As well as writing down a plan of action, take the time to picture it in your mind's eye. This gives you the opportunity to see how you will accomplish each step along the way. A creative and effective variation on this technique is to picture your goal as already having been achieved; and then you look backwards at the steps you took to achieve it.

This is how it's done:

    1. Close your eyes and imagine that you have already achieved your goal. You are feeling great. Perhaps you're now a non-smoker, a healthier person, or that you are running a successful business. Feel how good it is to have achieved your goal.

    2. Now look back at what you did. Picture the steps you took just before you achieved your goal, then the step before that, all the way back to the first step.

    3. Open your eyes and hold on to the good feeling of achievement.

When writing down your plan of action ask yourself the following questions:

- o What do I know about starting this goal?
- o What is it that I need and don't have right now that will allow me to achieve my goal?
- o What skills do I have in this field and what other skills do I need to learn?
- o Am I going about this in the best way or is there a better way?

o You can think about the possible challenges and obstacles and imagine dealing with each one effectively.

Step four - take small steps and decide on goals that are realistic

Your goals don't have to be big ones, because if you aim too high you may miss the mark. You may find it helpful to break your goals down into small steps. For instance, the goal: *"I want to lose 80 pounds in weight,"* may seem overwhelming. Instead, set goals in small increments by starting with the sub-goal of losing seven pounds. Decide on how you are going to change your eating habits – what kind of diet is the healthiest way to lose weight, should I discuss this with my doctor etc. Perhaps you can join a gym or go swimming. By breaking your goals into small realistic segments, you are far more likely to achieve them. In addition, you need to ask yourself if it's reasonable to achieve the goal you've set.

Alice wants to become a professional opera singer. She has spent a small fortune on singing lessons but she just doesn't have the voice for opera. In the end, the strain becomes too much. Her goal is just not working, so she decides to switch tracks and study music and acting at a theatre college. Alice failed to achieve her initial goal but she didn't give up. She identified her real need as wanting to work in music and she had the flexibility to switch goals, so she is now on the cusp of turning professional. If your goal doesn't seem to be working out, it may be an indication that it's time to change direction.

Dealing with the blocks to change

Earlier in this book, we saw how procrastination and perfectionism can block us from achieving our goals. Here are five false ideas that can also derail us and make our goals impossible to achieve.

False Idea 1
It will happen because I say so
It is wrong to believe that change will occur because you demand it. For instance, some people believe that it's enough to chant or repeat positive affirmations to effect change. While affirmations can be an effective way to build confidence and keep you thinking positively, they're very rarely enough.

Change requires practical work, perseverance and practise. As well as using affirmations, focus on the practical steps needed to effect change and then start doing them. For example, if you used the visualization technique described earlier in this chapter, start to put the steps you pictured into practise. The effort you put in will encourage you to take further steps until you achieve your goal.

False Idea 2

It's written in the stars and I am powerless to change things

Some people believe that their life is mapped out in the stars, and that they are powerless to do anything about it. If their daily horoscopes do not match their goals they give up. Even if you do believe that the stars play an influence in your life, any astrologer worth their salt will tell you that astrology shows indications and trends rather than what "must be." You have the power to make choices in your life. You can choose what to do and when to do it. That includes deciding on and fulfilling your goals.

False Idea 3

I must have the approval, love and encouragement of others before I can change

Sometimes people believe that in order to make a change in their life they must have the approval, love and support of others. It is very nice to have the support of other people, such as your partner or parents, but MUST you have their approval every time? After all, what happens if they disapprove? Does it mean you have to abandon your dream if they happen to disagree with your life choices?

It can be wise and helpful to seek the advice of others, and if people offer advice, take the time to evaluate it. However, you must make the final decision. Remember whose life it is and who's in charge of your destiny.

False Idea 4

I've always done it this way and it's impossible for me to change

Some people believe that they can never make a change and others think they need years of therapy to make significant improvements in their life. You may believe you are a creature of habit. However, habits are learned and can be unlearned. You can decide to change. By suspending cynicism and following the ideas and techniques in this book, you can prove to yourself that a change of habit is possible.

False Idea 5

I will never have the confidence to change

You may doubt your ability to achieve your goals or you may believe that you cannot handle mistakes. You may think that other people seem to have supreme self-confidence in everything they do. Confidence in your abilities can be learnt. Without running yourself down, be aware of the areas in your life where you lack experience and then decide to do something about it. Be realistic about your limits and what you can and cannot change. Next, make the decision to push yourself to the edge of your abilities. Be prepared to leave your comfort zone.

If you're anxious about making mistakes, recognise that you learn through making them. A mistake doesn't mean you are foolish, weak or stupid. It does mean that you are a fallible human being just like everyone else. Instead of worrying about what others think, analyse the mistake and, if possible, correct it. Don't be afraid to take calculated risks. Above all – persevere. This will propel you closer to achieving your goals.

Learn to tolerate frustration

The psychologist Dr Albert Ellis developed a concept he termed low frustration tolerance (LFT). This arises when a person experiences a frustrating situation or feeling and blows it way out of proportion.

He or she will have thoughts such as:

- *"I can't bear it"*
- *"I can't stand it"*
- *"This is awful"*
- *"This is terrible"*

If you have failed to stick to a diet, stop smoking or keep to an exercise program, then low frustration tolerance may be at the root of your broken goal.

You may believe that it's just too difficult to follow a diet and that you cannot stand the unpleasant feelings associated with abstaining from chocolate and cream cakes. Perhaps you experience a *"day from hell"* and believe you can't stand feeling upset. You tell yourself, *"This should not be happening to me,"* and get angry and depressed. Instead of dealing with your feelings, you medicate the emotions by overeating.

Have you ever heard yourself saying:

o   *"I must eat now."*

o   *"It's terrible to wait till dinnertime."*

o   *"I must have my daily fix of chocolate right NOW."*

The good news is you can learn to successfully cope with the unpleasant feelings of discomfort often associated with dieting.

Back to my consulting room, Stephanie is starting to become aware of how she sabotages her diet.

Stephanie: *"Just the other night I was out with my friend David. We were going to see a film and decided to have something to eat beforehand. For two weeks, I had been doing really well and knew exactly what to eat and what to avoid – but I still gave in."*

Michael: *"What happened?"*

Stephanie: *"I ordered a salad and baked potato. I ate it slowly and enjoyed the meal. After I finished, I was feeling satisfied. Then David asked to see the dessert menu. I also looked at the menu and saw profiteroles and cream – one of my favorite desserts."*

Michael: *"What thoughts were going through your mind at this point?"*

Stephanie: *"That it's just not fair. I should be able to have a nice dessert. I'm going to have those profiteroles – I deserve them after the day from hell I've just had."*

Michael: *"And what were the advantages of thinking like that?"*

Stephanie: *"Well, I suppose it meant I could eat the dessert I wanted. I felt good for about two minutes."*

Michael: *"Yes, it enabled you to justify why you should be allowed the dessert. That's a rationalization. What were the disadvantages of thinking like that?"*

Stephanie: *"Oh, lots. First, I felt guilt. I believed I blew my diet and that two weeks of hard work were for nothing. I didn't enjoy the film or the rest of the evening with David. I can now see that when similar situations have occurred in the past it can often take me about a month before I even attempt another diet."*

I explain to Stephanie that when working towards achieving a long-term goal there will almost inevitably be some hassles, such as emotional discomfort, along the way. Her restaurant experience with David is a prime example of that discomfort. Stephanie told herself, *"It's just not fair."* Consequently she made herself feel angry. She then went on to justify having a plate of profiteroles and cream because she had experienced a bad day at work. This had the effect of temporarily alleviating her discomfort but as a consequence contributed towards sabotaging her long-term goal of losing weight.

Stephanie: *"But I can't stand the feeling of not being able to have chocolate and cakes."*

Michael: *"If you want to successfully stick to your diet you need to challenge the notion that you should not have to feel discomfort. No one likes to feel discomfort but can it truly be said that you can't stand it? After all, if you truly couldn't stand something you would die. In reality, you can stand many things. What's the worst that could happen if you went without some unhealthy food for a while?"*

Stephanie: *"Well, when put like that, nothing terrible but how do I change it."*

After this conversation, I introduce Stephanie to two techniques:

Rational Coping Statements
Rational coping statements are assertions that you make to yourself to help you cope with and tackle difficult situations.

You can write coping statements down on a card and carry them around with you to use in challenging situations. You can use or modify Stephanie's coping statements or write your own.

Here are some of Stephanie's coping statements:

o *I don't need a cream cake when I am upset*

o *It's not awful sticking to a diet – just a bit uncomfortable sometimes*

o *I don't have to eat chocolate even when I have a strong urge to do so*

o *It's uncomfortable but not terrible - and I can stand it*

o *If I slip up on my diet that only proves I am a fallible, but still acceptable, human being*

o *I can still accept myself even when I make a mistake like eating the wrong food*

o *It's sometimes hard to stick to a diet but it's even harder when I don't*

Referenting

People who have a hard time breaking an unwanted habit will sometimes emphasize the advantages of continuing with the behaviour, and the disadvantages of changing the behaviour. The technique of referenting involves reversing this. In Stephanie's case, an example would involve writing down the advantages and pleasures of eating healthy foods and the disadvantages and negative consequences of continuing to eat unhealthy food.

These can then be reviewed several times a day, and like the rational coping statements, can be used in challenging situations.

138

Below is the list created by Stephanie. Although she uses the technique to deal with her diet-related problem, it can be adapted for any habit or problem behaviour you wish to change. The same applies for the coping statements.

The disadvantages of Stephanie continuing to eat in an unhealthy way:

- o Weight gain
- o Unhelpful irrational thinking
- o Disapproving of myself
- o Lack of energy
- o Damage to my health
- o Feeling bloated
- o Getting out of breath
- o Trouble exercising
- o Not being able to wear nice clothes

The advantages of Stephanie eating healthy foods and sticking to her diet:

- o Weight loss
- o Feeling better about myself
- o Improvement in health
- o More energy
- o Confidence when dating
- o Enthusiastic about exercise
- o Realistic thinking
- o Enjoying buying clothes again
- o Living longer

Stephanie finds it very helpful to go over the disadvantages of not staying on her diet and the advantages of sticking with it. She reads her lists vigorously to herself at least four times a day, especially at vulnerable times such as before eating and before entering a food shop. This, along with coping statements and the support from trusted friends, enables her to lose weight. Stephanie is now at a healthy, happy weight and has also stopped smoking. Using the ideas in this book, you can achieve your most treasured goals too.

Major Points

- Do not demand that you MUST achieve your goals every time. Instead, adopt the attitude that you're going to do the very best you can. If you make a mistake, view it as an opportunity for learning.
- Prioritise your goals by deciding which ones are most important to you. Write *one* for the most important, *two* for the next and so on. You may find it helpful to break your goals down into small steps.
- A good plan of action is important, or you may find your goals get confused. Knowing what steps you are going to take to reach your goal encourages lasting change.
- Picture yourself successfully achieving your goals in your imagination. This gives you the opportunity to see how you will accomplish each step along the way.
- List the advantages of sticking with and achieving your goals and the disadvantages of giving up on them. Then vigorously go over the lists whenever you feel disheartened.

From Head to Heart

I will set myself achievable, attainable goals.

Changing my behaviour may be uncomfortable at times but I can stand it.

I will work towards my goals, doing the best I can, but I won't demand perfection.

It is very nice to have the support of others, but that doesn't mean I MUST have it.

Staying Positive in a Crazy World

The reason people find it so hard to be happy is that they always see the past better than it was, the present worse than it is, and the future less resolved than it will be.
Marcel Pagnol

Maintaining a positive attitude can feel like an uphill battle in a world that seems full of obstacles. It's all too easy for negative ideas to cloud our minds and prevent us from achieving our goals. I hope this book has helped you see that our attitude towards ourselves, others and life in general does not have to remain set in stone. Enjoying a successful, happy and emotionally healthy life is within your grasp. Here's how to stay positive, in ten easy steps:

1. Keep track of your irrational thoughts and challenge them.

Life is tricky enough at times, without adding irrational beliefs into the mix. These unhelpful thoughts can wreak havoc. Not only do they make us unhappy, but they cause problems in all aspects of our lives. When holding an irrational belief, we are demanding that events and circumstances be different from the way they actually are. This is self-defeating and highly likely to cause emotional pain.

Whenever you feel upset about a situation, use the self-help form to discover what irrational beliefs may be influencing you. Then challenge and change those beliefs. Remember to challenge your irrational beliefs on a regular basis. On many occasions, you will not be personally responsible for upsetting situations. However, you can still take responsibility for the way you feel and how you respond to the event. Taking responsibility for the way you think, feel and act can seem like a challenge at times. However, the change in the way you react, behave and feel will make it worthwhile.

2. Learn to laugh at yourself

If you can laugh at yourself and your mistakes you'll experience far less worry and tension in your life. Indeed, laughter may truly be one of life's best medicines. There is research to suggest that laughter may protect you from heart disease and even heart attacks. The actor Paul Newman credited his ability to laugh at himself, and his reluctance to take himself too seriously, as the biggest factors behind his enormous success.

Humour is an effective coping mechanism that can lift you out of a negative mood and enable you to accept yourself and your foibles. Learning not to take yourself seriously and seeing the funny side of your mistakes will help you put them in perspective. There may be aspects of your physical features or personality that you don't like and cannot change. When these are viewed through humourous eyes, it can be easier to accept the things that cannot be changed.

3. Accept change as part of life and be flexible

Change can be difficult, stressful and even painful. However, change, like death and taxes, is inevitable. Whether you're moving house, being made redundant, starting a new job or having a baby, you can ease the stress of change by following these ideas:

A - Accept change

Change is inevitable, and sometimes there's not a lot you can do about it. However, you can do something about how you deal with the change. Instead of blowing the situation out of proportion, adopt the attitude that you can control the speed of change and your reactions to it. Adopt the attitude that change is a challenge rather than a threat.

145

Remember to use the strategies and techniques in this book, such as the self-help form.

B - Prepare for change

If you know that change is coming, you can prepare for it in advance. For instance, if you are going to start a new job, it may be wise to take a break after leaving your previous employment. Use the time to do research, learn about your new workplace, their products, culture, etc. Preparation for change will minimise stress and make the process easier to handle.

C - Seek out supporters of change

Sometimes people who are going through, or who have gone through, the same or similar issues can be helpful and supportive. Family, colleagues and friends can help you clarify your goals and feelings. Don't feel embarrassed about asking for help. As the saying goes, *"A problem shared is a problem halved."*

4. Leave your comfort zone and take sensible risks

Many of us tend to stay in our comfort zone rather than take risks. Your comfort zone is the area of familiarity where life feels safe and predictable. But the comfort zone can also be boring; it can lead to frustration and stop you from discovering new and exciting things about yourself, about others and about life. If you truly want to discover what you are capable of achieving, you need to leave the comfort zone and take some sensible risks.

146

When you stay in the comfort zone:

- o You only do things you know others will approve of.
- o You never try new things because it goes against your pre-existing ideas.
- o You avoid tasks where success is not guaranteed.

Leaving the comfort zone involves:

- o Trying new things when others may disapprove.
- o Trying something new even though it challenges your pre-existing beliefs.
- o Taking on new tasks where success is not guaranteed.

Risk-taking needs to be sensible and taken slowly. Avoid risks where there is a chance you could harm yourself or others.

Examples of risk-taking are:

- o Asking someone out on a date despite the risk of rejection.
- o Offering your opinion to a group of people at work.
- o Public speaking.
- o Learning something new.

A powerful technique developed by the psychologist Albert Ellis is called a shame-attacking exercise. The idea is to do something despite a fear of looking foolish or feeling embarrassed. The goal of this exercise is to learn that you can cope effectively with shame and embarrassment.

Examples of attacking shame involve:

- o Going into a shop lift and announcing the floor level aloud every time the lift stops.
- o Singing aloud in public.
- o Asking someone what year it is.

Do not do anything that could harm yourself or others. With practise, you'll discover that you can cope even if people disapprove of you or laugh at you. Sensible risk-taking is worthwhile and it can even be fun.

5. Resolve to look reality in the face

Reality, including unpleasant reality, is a fact. Sometimes circumstances do not allow our dreams to happen; at other times people let us down. Therefore, when we demand that things be different from the way they actually are, we give ourselves unpleasant feelings such as anger, fear and depression. This in turn can lead us to exaggerate the severity of a situation, turning a dislike into an unbearable horror.

If you find yourself demanding things MUST be different, ask yourself, *"Where is it written that things must be different from the way they actually are? It would be very nice if they were different but why MUST they be?"*

This is not to say that you shouldn't work at changing unpleasant situations, but by changing your demands into preferences, you will keep your unpleasant realities in perspective and you will be in a better position to achieve your goals.

If life gets a little too frustrating, you may need to adjust your attitude to make things easier. When we place unrealistic demands on ourselves, others and life, we feel frustrated and we waste time and energy that could be used more productively. By challenging our irrational beliefs, we take the pressure off and we are better able to go with the flow.

6. Learn to accept uncertainty

One thing is certain: there are no certainties in life. We may want to know for sure that an outcome will be positive, but sadly, there are no guarantees. When we find it hard to cope, uncertainty creates worry, fear and anxiety. Instead of demanding certainty, recognise that it is impossible to be certain about everything in life. Thinking about all the things that could go wrong won't give you any more control over your life. Persistently fantasising about worst-case scenarios won't keep bad things from happening. It's worth bearing in mind that it is possible to live with the fact that something could go wrong and still lead a happy life.

Create a "worry time". Set a regular time and place where you can worry. At that time and for 20 minutes every day, allow yourself to worry. During this time, worry about whatever is on your mind. If anxious thoughts and worries come to mind at other times of the day, tell yourself you will worry about them later during the allotted worry time. If you're concerned that you will forget your worries quickly, write them down. By postponing your worries, you break the habit of worrying during the day. This will give you a greater sense of control over your life.

7. Build and maintain your relationships

Developing and maintaining relationships with friends takes time and energy and, when it comes to your partner, it is likely to be a life-long commitment. It can be easy to assume that we know all there is to know about our partner, their thoughts, goals and intentions. It can then be a surprise to discover that our knowledge of them is incomplete. What follows are some tips that can help you build and maintain successful relationships with your friends and partner.

A - Be yourself:

"Just be yourself," sounds like a cliché. However, when you act in a way that you think the other person wants you to, you stop them from seeing the genuine *you*. Being yourself gives you and the other person the opportunity to

see if you're compatible and share the same interests, values, outlook, humour etc.

B - Use your communication skills:

Earlier in this book, you read about "I" and "you" statements. These communication skills are important to use in all relationships.

To recap: "You" statements are far more likely to cause the other person to become defensive. "I" statements are a way of communicating an issue without accusing the other person of being the problem. Contrast the following:

A. "You" statement - *"You never think things through."*

B. "I" statement - *"I would really like you to think before rushing into anything."*

Never fight by attacking your friend or partner. Instead, ask for specific changes in their behaviour.

C - Build bridges:

Good relationships are built on teamwork, co-operation and respect for each other's point of view. Conflicts are far easier to resolve when we are prepared to listen and compromise. By giving equal importance to the feelings and needs of the other person, we are far more likely to resolve a conflict. Lightening the load with a healthy dose of humour can also go a long way to resolving problems.

8. Take time out to relax

Do you make the mistake of thinking that you do not have the time to relax? Do you believe that winding down at

151

the end of a hard day is the only relaxation you need? Waiting for a stressful event to occur is not the best time to begin learning relaxation. It's far better to set aside 20 minutes a day for practise. Once learnt, you will be able to let go of your tension in virtually any situation. Relaxation produces a wonderful feeling of well being, and it helps to relax tense muscles.

Two Relaxation Techniques

Brief relaxation

Techniques such as self-hypnosis, mindfulness, meditation and yoga can be extremely useful in reducing stress and tension. You can also benefit from learning a brief method of relaxation. This is especially helpful if you find yourself in a stressful situation that requires you to let go of tension immediately. You can also practise the technique for a couple of minutes every two or three hours to keep stress at bay. All you need to do is:

1. Sit in a comfortable chair
2. Relax and close your eyes
3. Focus on the rhythm of your breathing
4. Let your whole body become loose and limp
5. Imagine a relaxing scene

Breathe your stress away

When a person feels under threat their breathing rate increases in preparation for the fight or flight response, but if this response is inappropriate, then one can feel anxious and short of breath. In order to achieve a good quality of relaxation, you need to learn how to breathe correctly. This may surprise you. After all, you have been breathing since you were born. Many people who experience stress and anxiety are breathing in a shallow way from their chest. People who are relaxed are breathing slowly and deeply from their abdomen. An effective way of switching off stress and anxiety is to practise deep breathing.

Here's how it's done:

1. Sit down in a comfortable place
2. Tune into the rhythm of your breathing
3. Put your hand on your stomach. As you breathe, try to feel your stomach moving up and down. The aim is to breathe from your stomach instead of from your chest
4. Slow down the rate of your breathing

At first, you may find it difficult to breathe from your stomach. To get a comfortable rhythm you may find it helpful to say the word *"relax"* as you breathe out. As you keep practising, you will find your body becoming more relaxed

9. Work to live: don't live to work

Many people find it difficult to maintain the correct balance between their work, relaxation and enjoyment.

Work is what you do in order to earn a living. Taking breaks during your day will improve your concentration. Eating when you take a break will help you to regain and maintain your energy. Adding variety to your working day can also help. Of course, the extent to which you will be able to do this will depend on your work circumstances. However, getting away from your working environment when you get a break is important. Try something different at this time, such as going for a walk, using a relaxation technique, phoning an acquaintance or going out for lunch with a friend. Add some variety – it's the spice of life.

Pursue outside interests:

Hobbies can be a good pastime as they can help you to get away from it all. They have therapeutic value, reduce stress, enhance creativity and keep the mind active. As well as a hobby, other pursuits can contribute towards a balanced life. For instance, you may choose to give something back by doing some form of voluntary work. The value of this can be immense. For example, some voluntary work can be challenging and therefore be a useful way of learning to overcome difficulties. This can increase your confidence, and this can be carried through to other areas of your life.

Pursuits can include but are not limited to: Sport, concerts, cooking classes, studying, DIY, learning a musical instrument, going to the beach, dancing, gardening, singing, cinema, theatre, amateur dramatics, book clubs, politics, creative writing, rambling, martial arts, yoga, meditation, and many more.

10. Accept yourself – as you are

I end this book where it began, by stating that unconditional self-acceptance is very different from self-esteem. In our society, we tend to base our self-worth on our abilities and accomplishments.

Consider these two statements:

A. *"I am a good person because I do well."*

B. *"I can accept myself even when I make mistakes."*

I hope this book has pointed out the problems associated with the first of these statements, and shown it is best to accept yourself.

REMEMBER – Refuse to rate yourself, your soul or your essence! Instead, rate things *about* yourself. Accept yourself unconditionally, in spite of your shortcomings and strive to change what you can.

I wish you well.

From Head to Heart

I choose to accept myself unconditionally.

Things are never really as bad or terrible as I think they are.

I am calm, secure and relaxed.

Making a mistake does not make me a mistake.

Mistakes are just mistakes.

<u>SELF HELP FORM</u>

A. Activating Event

B. Irrational Beliefs

C. Consequences

D. Disputing

E. Effective New Thinking

F. New Feelings and Actions

(For extra self-help forms, please photocopy)

RECOMMENDED READING

For the Challenges of Life
Identifying, Understanding and Solutions to Stress
Michael Cohen. Caxton Editions

How to Cope When the Going Gets Tough
Dr Windy Dryden and Jack Gordon. Sheldon Press

For Emotional Misery and Depression
The Feeling Good Handbook
David Burns MD. Penguin Books Ltd

Overcoming Depression
Dr Paul Gilbert. Constable and Robinson

For Anxiety and Fear
Master Your Panic and Take Back Your Life
Denise F Beckfield PH.D. Impact

When Panic Attacks: The New Drug-Free Anxiety Therapy That Can Change Your Life
David Burns. Broadway Books

For Confidence and Self-Acceptance
Hold Your Head Up
Paul Hauck. Sheldon Press

Building Self-Confidence for Dummies
Kate Burton. John Wiley & Sons

Relationships and Assertiveness
Your Perfect Right
Robert Alberti PH.D and Michael Emmons PH.D. Impact

Better Relationships: Practical Ways to Make Your Love Last
Sarah Litvinoff. Vermillion

Useful websites
If you would like to know more about Cognitive Behaviour Therapy and Clinical Hypnotherapy then the following websites may be of use.

In The UK
Michael Cohen (author and therapist)
www.hypnosisandhealing.co.uk

British Association for Behavioural and Cognitive Psychotherapies
www.babcp.com
The Association for Rational Emotive Behaviour Therapy
http://www.arebt.org

National Council for Hypnotherapy.
www.hypnotherapists.org.uk

In the USA
Beck Institute for Cognitive Therapy and Research
www.beckinstitute.org

The Albert Ellis Institute
www.rebt.org

National Guild of Hypnotists
www.ngh.net

Index

Acknowledgements

With thanks to Marianne Makdisi, Jackie Simons, Lisa Lee and to my family for their help and encouragement.

Michael Cohen is a Cognitive Behavioural Hypnotherapist and runs a busy practice based in London. He has 25 years experience in one-to-one therapy and in running workshops. Michael has made many radio and television appearances and is featured frequently in the national press. He is also the author of *Identifying Understanding and Solutions to Stress*.

Lightning Source UK Ltd.
Milton Keynes UK
UKHW01f1819070918
328516UK00012B/752/P

9 780956 517760